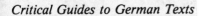
Critical Guides to German Texts

6 Fontane: Effi Briest

Critical Guides to German Texts

EDITED BY MARTIN SWALES

FONTANE

Effi Briest

Stanley Radcliffe

Senior Lecturer in German
University of Bristol

Grant & Cutler Ltd
1986

© Grant & Cutler Ltd
    1986
ISBN 0 7293 0260 1
LC Catalog Card No. 86-82406
(CIP applied for)

I.S.B.N. 84-599-1867-X

DEPÓSITO LEGAL: V. 95 - 1987

Printed in Spain by
Artes Gráficas Soler, S.A., Valencia
for
GRANT & CUTLER LTD
55-57, GREAT MARLBOROUGH STREET, LONDON W1V 2AY
and
27 SOUTH MAIN STREET, WOLFEBORO, NH 03894-2069, USA

Contents

Prefatory Note   7

1. Fact into Fiction   9

2. 'Eine Geschichte mit Entsagung'   14

3. Portrait of a Society   26

4. Marietta Trippelli and the Limits of Independence   33

5. The 'Spuk'   39

6. A Sense of Place   49

7. Conversational Variations   54

8. The Crampas Letters   61

9. Form and Style   68

10. Critical Reception and Literary Assessment   72

Select Bibliography   80

Prefatory Note

The page numbers in brackets in this text refer to pages of *Effi Briest*, which is volume 17 of the *Werke und Schriften* in the Ullstein-published *Fontane Bibliothek*, based on the edition by Walter Keitel and Helmuth Nürnberger, originally published by Hanser.

Articles in the Jolles-Festschrift: *Formen realistischer Erzählkunst* are referred to under *Jolles*. Other references, indicated in brackets by italicised figures, are to the numbered items in the Select Bibliography.

1. Fact into Fiction

Fontane's regular association with the polite social world of Berlin brought much gossip to his ears and in this way he was presented with the material for numerous works, including *Effi Briest*. 'Presented' is the appropriate term in the latter instance, for his informant, Emma Lessing, wife of the proprietor of the *Vossische Zeitung*, recounting a recent scandal involving a mutual acquaintance, suggested its suitability for development into a novel. The subject of the gossip was a Baron Armand Léon von Ardenne and his wife Elisabeth, née von Plotho. Fontane had actually met this couple over dinner at Emma Lessing's house in 1880.

The personal history that lies behind Fontane's story was only fully established in 1963, when Hans Werner Seiffert was able to piece it together from the papers of the Ardenne family (pp.310-315). Baron von Ardenne, an officer in the Zieten Hussars, based at Rathenow (north of Berlin) had in 1873 at the age of twenty-four married the nineteen-year-old Elisabeth von Plotho, from a nearby estate at Parcy on the Elbe. At first the marriage was successful but Ardenne increasingly neglected his young wife in the pursuit of his military career. Transferred to the garrison at Düsseldorf in 1881, he and his wife engaged in a busy social life, particularly among artistic and dramatic enthusiasts. With one of these Elisabeth soon found herself becoming deeply involved. Emil Hartwich, a local magistrate, unhappily married, was strongly attracted to the vivacious young *Baronin*, with whom he shared a love of the theatre. A secret correspondence begun at this time continued after the return of Ardenne and his wife to Berlin, where Ardenne served on the general staff. Hartwich paid periodic visits to Berlin, and in the summer of 1886, while Ardenne (now a colonel) was on manoeuvres, Hartwich and Elisabeth planned to elope and eventually marry. However, Ardenne's suspicions were by now aroused and, using a key of his own, he opened his wife's writing case and discovered letters from Hartwich. A challenge to a duel was the immediate outcome and Hartwich, though an excellent pistol shot, was mortally wounded in the duel which was fought at Bonn on 27 November 1886. Ardenne divorced his wife in March 1887. He went on to become a general and died in 1919 in Berlin, but Elisabeth lived to the ripe old age of ninety-nine, dying at Lindau in 1952 after engaging for many years in charitable work.

The events were very recent and had been widely reported in the press. If Fontane was to make literary use of them, they clearly had to be disguised. Names and circumstances had to be changed, and a shift of locality also seemed desirable. It was in any case Fontane's practice to strike a middle line between precise adherence to the facts of a case and pure invention. The known facts provided a sound base on which a *representative* history could be built by the addition of further typical features of life in the social world with which Fontane was so familiar.

The outline sketch of his novel was rapidly written down, as though dictated by some external impulse — 'wie mit dem Psychographen' (letter of 11 November 1895). Progress was then halted for some considerable time: Fontane was in some difficulty over the nature of the changes that were needed. A prolonged spell of ill-health added to his problems, for it produced a state of depression that was detrimental to composition.

The scene of the action and the names of the characters were changed several times before the story as it now exists emerged. Presumably in an attempt to move as far as possible from the real-life Rhineland setting, Fontane first located the action in Prussian areas of western Poland, but finally moved to the Brandenburg/Pomeranian region with which he was so intimately acquainted. Authenticity of detail was thus guaranteed (*14*, p.128).

Finding names seems to have caused few problems. Hohen-Cremmen probably derives from Kremmen, a small town some twenty-five miles north of Berlin: Fontane locates it in the 'Ländchen Friesack', in Westhavelland (letter of 29 May 1894). The family name of Briest was familiar to Fontane from his historical studies of Brandenburg and may even have been suggested by a village of that name in the Magdeburg area from which the real Effi originated. The name Effi, slow to emerge, seems to have been a chance prompting: Fontane found its vowel sounds especially appealing: 'für mein Gefühl sehr hübsch, weil viel e und i darin ist; das sind die beiden feinen Vokale' (letter of 9 November 1893). The Bellingsche Haus (home of Effi's grandparents) is in the village of Belling, just north of Pasewalk.

The switch of location to 'Kessin' on the Baltic coast is especially significant. The bout of illness which prevented Fontane from progressing from his initial draft of 1889 seemed to presage the end of his career as a writer: he was, after all, now over seventy years of age. The unexpected breakthrough came with the writing of the autobiographical *Meine Kinderjahre* in the winter of 1892. Childhood recollections stimulated vivid memories of his life in Swinemünde between the ages of eight and thirteen, and the Baltic port was now invested with the literary identity of 'Kessin'. His spirits remarkably recovered, Fontane resumed the writing of *Effi Briest*, which was completed in May 1894.

What actually seems to have sparked off the writing of the novel was not the episode of the discovered letters and the duel, but the paradox of Effi being summoned from childhood play in the garden to meet her appointed husband: 'Die ganze Geschichte … hätte, als mir Frau Lessing davon erzählte, weiter keinen großen Eindruck auf mich gemacht, wenn nicht … die Szene bez. die Worte: "Effi komm" darin vorgekommen wären … (sie machte) *solchen* Eindruck auf mich, daß aus *dieser* Szene die ganze lange Geschichte entstanden ist.' (letter of 21 February 1896).

The age gap between husband and wife is widened in Fontane's novel: Fontane thus establishes a more credible basis for their emotional incompatability and for Innstetten's greater familiarity with the ways of the world. That he exchanges the roles of the two men, presenting the seducer as an army officer and the deceived husband as a civil servant may have been designed to help cover his tracks: it does at the same time

increase the verisimilitude of the story, the army officer being a
traditional seducer figure, while the civil servant Innstetten is
more readily accepted as the stickler for protocol and routine.

Other quite separate experiences of Fontane found a place
naturally in his developing scenario. Effi's appearance and dress
are a case in point. While staying in the Harz town of Thale
during the early stages of composition, Fontane was sitting on
the balcony one evening when a young Englishman and his sister
(aged about fifteen) appeared:

> '... Das Mädchen war genau so gekleidet, wie ich Effi in
> den allerersten und dann auch wieder in den allerletzten
> Kapiteln geschildert habe: Hänger, blau und weiß
> gestreifter Kattun, Ledergürtel und Matrosenkragen. Ich
> glaube, daß ich für meine Heldin keine bessere
> Erscheinung und Einkleidung finden konnte ...' (letter of 2
> March 1895).

Elements that derive from boyhood memories of Swinemünde
are recognised when we read his autobiographical *Meine
Kinderjahre*: their integration into the work seems remarkably
uncontrived, so neatly do they fit. The *Apotheke* which
Fontane's family occupied in Swinemünde had enormous attic
rooms, one of which was said to be haunted by a local man
executed for murder. Fontane reports how he used to lie awake
at night listening to frightening sounds coming from the room
above him, attributed by his father to cats. From the ceiling of
one of the lower rooms hung a stuffed turbot — undoubtedly
the prototype of the shark and crocodile that hang in the hall of
the *Landrat*'s house at Kessin.

The description of a clearing in the dunes opening to the sea,
where a murderer was executed in spring 1828 is remarkably
similar to that in which the duel takes place between Innstetten
and Crampas, while a visit to an *Oberförster* in the hinterland,
followed by a hazardous homeward journey, must surely be
more than coincidentally similar to the visit to Oberförster Ring
and the return journey through the *Schloon*. Fontane's mother
was ill at the time of the family's move to Swinemünde and had

gone to Berlin for medical attention (forerunner of Frau von Briest?): her personal drawing-room was furnished and decorated by her husband in preparation for her arrival, just as was Effi's at Kessin. The account of the social world that confronted the Fontane family could almost stand in the pages of the novel itself; the tight-knit society of Kessin is suggested in all its stark exactness. The names of certain leading families, e.g. the Flemmings and the Borckes, also recur in Fontane's novel, and the pattern of social events throughout the year is reported almost in identical formulation.

Like Kessin's physical environment, characters too seem to derive elements from this autobiographical sketch — though many stripes are exchanged for spots. The figure of the nurse, Roswitha, has certain traits in common with the Fontanes' servant Schröder, a woman of most unprepossessing appearance but highly efficient and with a heart of gold. She regularly took the side of Fontane's mother in her disputes with her husband. Even Innstetten's somewhat tame *Brautbriefe* seem to owe something to Fontane senior's decidedly lukewarm addresses to his own bride: although Frau Fontane had kept these letters, they occasioned only bitter-sweet memories. 'Sie litt darunter', reports Fontane, 'daß mein Vater, so sehr er sie liebte, von Zärtlichkeitsallüren auch nie eine Spur gehabt hatte'.

A more appealing aspect of his father is incorporated in the character of Gieshübler (also a chemist), with his passion for reading newspapers and marking significant passages in them. Characters thus slowly coalesced from manifold, unrelated elements of Fontane's own experience. But Fontane did not simply 'lift' his material from life: he modified and integrated it meaningfully to fit the articulation of his plot.

2. 'Eine Geschichte mit Entsagung'

The point is well made by Sasse (*14*, p.127) that Effi's fate is determined less by her character than by purely circumstantial and extraneous factors. Questions of personal guilt and responsibility are thus to a considerable extent put out of court, but the degree of Effi's complicity in her fate can still legitimately be investigated.

Effi's opening comment to her childhood friends at Hohen-Cremmen: 'Eine Geschichte mit Entsagung ist nie schlimm' (p.10) is a testimony to her totally naive, inexperienced view of the world. Effi's character has been shaped by heredity and environment, and although Fontane does not present her in the manner of contemporary Naturalism, he nevertheless advances the appropriate evidence, with somewhat more subtle artistry than the latter's 'photographic' realism (he strongly disapproved of Naturalism's unconcern for artistic form and selection).

Essentially, Effi is characterised in the opening chapters of the novel, when we first meet her playing childhood games. A very uncomplicated sixteen-year-old, her chief delights include hide-and-seek and riding on the swing, and she wears a child's sailor-type outfit popular at that time. Effi's life thus far has been a simple round of play, congenial domestic tasks and healthy activity. Challenges seldom arise in a sheltered community like Hohen-Cremmen, and her education and upbringing have likewise not confronted her with difficult issues. Educated in the local school, Effi is less well informed than most of Fontane's young aristocratic heroines: she is to experience her intellectual inadequacy not only in the company of Innstetten (who embarks on a cultural crash-course for her during their honeymoon and later reads to her from his many 'sehr gute Bücher' (p.293), for she has still read very little), but also with Crampas and Marietta Tripelli.

Social attitudes and priorities absorbed in the home have been reinforced by Pastor Niemeyer's teaching. The desired prospect is to make a good marriage, advancing oneself socially, and to provide for the continuation of the family line. Guards officers offer the principal prospect (mostly sons of landowners themselves), and are universally sought after as dancing partners, escorts and companions. Many are imported for Effi's wedding celebrations. Effi's statement to her friends has been much quoted: 'Jeder ist der Richtige. Natürlich muß er von Adel sein und eine Stellung haben und gut aussehen' (p.20). Innstetten fits the image nicely: Effi has already referred to him approvingly: 'er ist Landrat, gute Figur und sehr männlich' (p.10). Her father, we note, likes his men 'männlich' (p.10), while her mother sees in Innstetten's proposal a chance to realise, through her daughter, the prospect she turned down twenty years previously.

Fontane writes of Effi 'In allem, was sie tat, paarte sich Übermut und Grazie' (p.8). The 'Grazie' in Effi is emphasised by her mother ('eigentlich hättest du doch wohl Kunstreiterin werden müssen', p.8) who sees only her own childhood image in Effi and has resisted the option of making 'eine Dame' out of her (p.9): she prefers to present her to Innstetten unkempt and unspoilt, just as she comes from her play in the garden. The engagement achieved, Effi returns to her play, as though a simple business transaction has been concluded. To the question of her feelings towards Innstetten, she replies with disarming lack of discrimination:

Warum soll ich ihn nicht lieben? Ich liebe Hulda, und ich liebe Bertha, und ich liebe Hertha. Und ich liebe auch den alten Niemeyer. Und daß ich euch liebe, davon spreche ich gar nicht erst. Ich liebe alle, die's gut mit mir meinen und gütig gegen mich sind und mich verwöhnen (p.34)

The *Übermut* in Effi expresses itself here with frank and self-centred directness. The world exists for her enjoyment of it, and her response is that of universal affection. The indulgence of her idiosyncrasies is a basic requirement, in the exercise of which she also relishes the sensation of danger: 'Ich klettre lieber, und ich

schaukle mich lieber, und am liebsten immer in der Furcht, daß
es irgendwo reißen oder brechen und ich niederstürzen könnte'
(p.34).

'Nicht so wild, Effi, nicht so leidenschaftlich' her mother cries
as Effi embraces her 'stürmisch' (p.9). An enormous zest for life
and adventure speaks from all her actions, but it has not been
channelled into meaningful activity. Effi consequently devotes
her thoughts to totally fanciful prospects. At a performance of
Cinderella shortly before her marriage, she finds the last act
especially appealing, as the heroine wakes up to find herself a
princess, or at least a countess: 'wirklich, es war ganz wie ein
Märchen' (p.27). She longs for her own future to correspond to
this *Märchen* tradition, and paints an utterly fanciful picture of
'life at the top', 'immer dicht neben der großen Mittelloge'
(p.32). The desire to be at the centre of attention is striking, and
she manifestly is the leader of her childhood companions.

The theme of 'etwas Apartes', frequently associated with Effi,
is seen by all critics as a vital aspect of her characterisation. Its
first mention occurs during the preparations for her marriage.
Leaving all the conventional purchases to her mother, she concerns herself only with special acquisitions, insisting here on 'nur
das Eleganteste': and if she has a real requirement, 'so mußte
dies immer was ganz Apartes sein. Und *darin* war sie anspruchs-
voll' (p.24). Her requests for wedding gifts are indeed of a
singular nature: a Japanese bed-screen, 'schwarz und goldene
Vögel darauf, alle mit einem langen Kranichschnabel', and a
bedside lamp 'mit rotem Schein' (p.30). Bance (*Jolles*, p.413)
detects erotic motifs here: the red light in particular has
associations with illicit sex, and Frau Briest hurriedly directs
Effi's thoughts into other channels:

> Du bist ein Kind. Schön und poetisch. Das sind so
> Vorstellungen. Die Wirklichkeit ist anders, und oft ist es
> gut, daß es statt Licht und Schimmer ein Dunkel gibt.
>   (pp.30-31)

The avoidance of challenging issues is not just the prerogative of
Herr von Briest, with his 'zu weites Feld'; it is her mother's

approach to the world also.

Effi's lack of serious purpose is stressed by images of lightness and air: 'eigentlich hättest du doch wohl Kunstreiterin werden müssen', her mother tells her as she exercises in the garden, 'Immer am Trapez, immer Tochter der Luft' (p.8). The theme is maintained later in Effi's delight in horse-riding or gliding over the snow in Innstetten's sleigh. When a flagpole is to be installed in the Hohen-Cremmen garden, she demands to be the first to ascend and attach the flag (p.15). Her expectations of life in Kessin are correspondingly naive; she feels she will need thick winter coats for this 'foreign' clime (some fifty miles further north), but anticipates the continuation of carefree enjoyment, especially in the dances on the Swedish steamers which she plans to attend with her guards-officer cousin Dagobert.

A confusion of priorities — commitment to social rank versus self-indulgence — is already rooted in Effi and emerges from the words to her mother:

Liebe kommt zuerst, aber gleich hinterher kommt Glanz und Ehre, und dann kommt Zerstreuung — ja, Zerstreuung, immer was Neues, immer was, daß ich lachen oder weinen muß. Was ich nicht aushalten kann, ist Langeweile. (p.32)

Innstetten has sensed this duality very early, when he tells her in Kessin: 'Du bist eine reizende kleine Frau, aber Festigkeit ist nicht eben deine Spezialität' (p.164).

In the indulgent parental home no hard and fast rules of life have been instilled into Effi; Innstetten's strict firmness of purpose is therefore frightening to her ('ich fürchte mich vor ihm', p.35), and a sense of inadequacy accompanies her into her marriage.

Effi leaves Hohen-Cremmen to confront a totally strange world in the society of Kessin. Circumstance and chance thus come into play to test the degree of her fitness for the role she has assumed, and her ability to make appropriate choices in life. The magnitude of her undertaking and the strength of will which it will require are matters beyond her present conception. Her first test comes on the very day after her arrival in Kessin, when, alone and aged just seventeen, she has to discharge the role of hostess. Her handling of the bashful Alonzo Gieshübler is so unconstrained and sympathetic that she wins him for life. She senses the fairy-tale quality of his devotion (p.65), and this, plus the excitement of the quite new world of Kessin, enables her to apply herself to the task of being a *Landrat*'s wife. She fits herself into her husband's work schedule and social visiting, and even accepts his refusal to move house because of the supposed haunting of their present one. The sacrifices seem worthwhile in the interests of promotion and a brighter future. She admits the going is dull but insists that she is at least as ambitious as Innstetten: 'Und dann wollen wir ja auch höher hinauf. Ich sage wir, denn ich bin eigentlich begieriger danach als du ...' (p.78). Critics generally have understressed the element of social ambition in Effi, endowing her with a mainly passive role. It is a vital and consistent strand in her make-up, and a principal reason for her rejection of her cousin Dagobert, whom she likes well enough, but finds too 'dalbrig' (p.181) — garrulous and inconsequential.

In return for her sacrifices, Effi has the right to expect openness and trust from her husband. It is Innstetten who in the event fails this test. On several occasions he keeps back information from Effi, suggesting a lack of confidence in her. The supposed haunting of the house is the most notable instance, Innstetten restraining himself from a full account of the relevant facts (p.57), and subsequently failing to carry out the undertaking to deal with the offending curtains in the upstairs room. At the same time he insists that Effi must take him on trust and agree that a move of house would damage his image and their joint prospects. Effi is forced to repress her fears and can only give them expression when she writes to Hohen-Cremmen, when she begs her mother not to let Innstetten know of them. Reservations thus begin to set in on both sides.

From time to time Effi reproaches Innstetten with his inattentiveness towards her. Whenever he indulges her she is genuinely appreciative. She enjoys her outings with him and

longs for more of his company. But for much of the time he is
abstracted and undemonstrative: each evening a ritual of rather
perfunctory affection is engaged in by Innstetten, which Effi
barely bothers to respond to (p.108). She is not always so
resigned: 'Nur einen Kuß könntest du mir geben. Aber daran
denkst du nicht. Auf dem ganzen weiten Weg nicht gerührt,
frostig wie ein Schneemann', she exclaims on their return from
their depressing social rounds (p.67). Herr von Briest knows his
daughter well and has already foreseen the likely consequences:
'Das wird eine Weile so gehen, ohne viel Schaden anzurichten,
aber zuletzt wird sie's merken, und dann wird es sie beleidigen
...' (p.40).

Yet love, in terms of total self-surrender, is beyond Effi's
powers too. Her affair with Crampas is to confirm this and
reinforces the indications already given by Fontane of her self-
centredness. The desire to be indulged continues as strongly as it
existed in her life at Hohen-Cremmen. There is a failure too to
cast off childhood associations and enter fully into her marriage.
Herr von Briest complains even after Innstetten's promotion to
Berlin, of Effi's comparative unconcern for her husband and
child, and continuing strong attachment to the childhood world
of Hohen-Cremmen. We note the delight she experiences in
visiting her old home and her reluctance to depart again. The
theme of *Heim* is never far from her thoughts, and in moments
of dejection she conjures it up, in an escape into happy
memories; and it is Hohen-Cremmen that finally provides the
peace that she seeks after the breaking of her marriage.

Innstetten, afraid of his own emotions, cannot effect the
necessary change in Effi: 'du bist eigentlich ... ein Zärtlichkeits-
mensch', she tells him. 'Du willst es bloß nicht zeigen und
denkst, es schickt sich nicht und verdirbt einem die Karriere'
(p.122). Preoccupation with his public image and society's
requirement of *Ordnung* is already too engrained to be significantly modified, and his promise to try to improve is not
implemented. The one moment in his life when emotion
apparently ruled him was in his proposal of marriage to Effi's
mother: that was some twenty years ago, and his rejection in
favour of a better match seems to have caused some bitterness

and led to a resolve to concentrate rigorously on the pursuit of material goals (p.13) — the 'Liebesgeschichte mit Entsagung' (p.10). Commentators largely pass over this episode from Innstetten's past — a past about which we learn remarkably little in the novel, yet the episode is rich in implication.

Effi herself reveals more of her own conditioning when Innstetten confesses to finding in her 'was Verführerisches'. 'Ach, mein einziger Geert', she replies, 'das ist ja herrlich, was du da sagst; nun wird mir erst recht wohl ums Herz ... Weißt du denn, daß ich mir das immer gewünscht habe? Wir müssen verführerisch sein, sonst sind wir gar nichts ...' (p.123). The use of the pronoun 'wir' stresses her belief in a collective feminine strategy, in a trivialised approach to life. It is surely ironical that Crampas should make his entry at this point.

Effi is flattered by Crampas' attentions and fascinated by his dangerous conversation. He now replaces Gieshübler as a contrast figure to Innstetten, indicating a shift in Effi's ethical adjustment. Innstetten, at times compelled by duty to abandon Effi to Crampas' company, is an honourable man and devoted to Effi, and has an infinite trust in her loyalty. Not to concede these indulgences would seem tyrannical of him. He warns Effi of the sort of person that Crampas is, but perhaps only adds piquancy to the sense of risk which Effi has always savoured (e.g. pp.147 and 164). The opportunity for Crampas' declaration of love is created by Innstetten's thoughtless desire to show his resoluteness and adventurousness in the encounter with the *Schloon* — though some other opportunity would doubtless have been exploited by Crampas.

Effi has been finding it increasingly difficult to resist Crampas' advances. Already, when talking to Gieshübler about the play in which she is to appear and which Crampas is to direct, she has conceded her subservience to his will: 'der Major hat so was Gewaltsames, er nimmt einem die Dinge gern über den Kopf fort. Und man muß dann spielen, wie er will, und nicht wie man selber will'. 'Sie sprach so noch weiter', adds Fontane, 'und verwickelte sich immer mehr in Widersprüche' (p.144). After the sleigh-ride episode, Effi admits to herself that she is lost: the desire to resist is undermined by her weakness of will: 'ihr fehlte die Nachhaltigkeit, und alle guten Anwandlungen gingen wieder vorüber ... Das Verbotene, das Geheimnisvolle hatte seine Macht über sie' (p.169). Her naive faith in some divine act of rescue has also evaporated — no 'Gottesmauer' has arisen to protect her (p.162).

She remembers the forthright words of Frau von Padden: 'worauf es ankommt, meine liebe junge Frau, das ist das Kämpfen. Man muß immer ringen mit dem natürlichen Menschen' (p.166). But Effi does not stem from such a strict and self-denying tradition, and the 'natürlicher Mensch' triumphs — as with all events in which Effi is a participant. She is a consistently drawn portrait.

The degree of Effi's guilt must be measured against the attitudes of others. Her own evalutation of her actions also undergoes change as her life is modified by events. A powerful sense of guilt fills her at first ('Meine Schuld ist sehr schwer', p.190), as she seeks to re-create her relationship with the unsuspecting Innstetten. She almost betrays herself in certain moments of unguarded comment, and here it is Innstetten's generous nature which comes to her rescue, dismissing as unworthy the suspicions that rise in his mind (pp.182-83). Fontane intended him to be seen in a positive light, as his comment in a letter shows: 'eigentlich ist er ... in jedem Anbetracht ein ganz ausgezeichnetes Menschenexemplar, dem es an dem, was man lieben muß, durchaus nicht fehlt' (27 October 1895).

The feigned illness which keeps Effi in Berlin is only one of a number of deceptions to which she must resort, and the village of Crampas on the island of Rügen is a sobering reminder of a past that will never completely fade. She strives to make amends ('In jeglichem, was sie tat, lag etwas Wehmütiges, wie eine Abbitte', p.207), and though forced to proceed with caution, feels happier and more relaxed, even confiding to her mother that she is now 'über den Berg' and fully content with her marriage to Innstetten, whom she designates 'der beste Mensch, etwas zu alt für sie und zu gut für sie' (p.216). This continuing affection for Innstetten is disregarded by some critics, who insist on seeing him as a quite unsuitable partner for Effi and their marriage as a total failure, above all Sasse (*14*, pp.131 and 135). Essentially it differs but little from that of her parents, as Pascal points out (*9*, p.202), and doubtless many others of their class.

Effi's disquiet stems primarily from the fact that she must engage in deception:

> Ja, Angst quält mich und dazu Scham über mein Lügenspiel. Aber Scham über meine Schuld, die hab' ich *nicht* oder doch nicht so recht oder doch nicht genug, und das bringt mich um, daß ich sie nicht habe. Wenn alle Weiber so sind, dann ist es schrecklich, und wenn sie nicht so sind, wie ich hoffe, dann steht es schlecht um mich, dann ist etwas nicht in Ordnung in meiner Seele, dann fehlt mir das richtige Gefühl. (p.219)

This struggle to come up to society's standards, to put her life 'in Ordnung', indicates the dominance of the collective in her thinking. Its code of behaviour has already been applied by her to others considered guilty of social misconduct, especially Roswitha with her 'sinful' past and mild flirtation with the coachman Kruse (p.177), but including also the unconventional Pastor Trippel (p.86) and likewise, it seems, Inspektor Pink at Hohen-Cremmen, involved with the gardener's wife (p.25). Marietta Trippelli herself is only just excluded (p.189). The irony of fate now requires Effi to condemn her own actions, yet privately she is not convinced of her unmitigated guilt.

With the discovery of the letters and her rejection by Innstetten, the situation changes radically. Now it is Innstetten who, by his lack of charity, puts her past deeds into a better light. She had come to rely on his affection, and that of her newly-found Berlin friends. Now a wall is built that excludes her totally from them. A numbed acquiescence is her first reaction, for, as a disgraced woman, she is powerless to act in her defence. Only the arrival of another 'fallen woman', Roswitha, to share her social exile rescues Effi from outright despair.

Effi's commitment to life slowly revives and with it the desire to be reconciled with her daughter, agonisingly reinforced by her chance sighting of Annie. Her continuing sense of shame restrains her from an immediate public reunion (p.269), but a private meeting is contrived by manipulating Innstetten's desire to please his seniors (p.271). The meeting, a total disaster, reveals to Effi the vengeful quality of the world she has offended. Where she has striven to make amends, society has striven to remember her offence. The question of guilt now assumes a different alignment. Effi's moral sense is outraged by Innstetten's conditioning of their daughter so that she rejects her own mother's affectionate approach. She experiences a moral superiority to this society which has seen fit to judge and condemn her:

> ich will meine Schuld nicht kleiner machen, ... aber *das* ist zuviel. Denn das hier, mit dem Kind, das bist nicht *du*, Gott, der mich strafen will, das ist *er*, bloß er! Ich habe geglaubt, daß er ein edles Herz habe und habe mich immer klein neben ihm gefühlt; aber jetzt weiß ich, daß *er* es ist, *er* ist klein. Und weil er klein ist, ist er grausam. Alles, was klein ist, ist grausam. (p.275)

For the first time in her life she feels superior to Innstetten. It is not God's hand that is seen at work here, but a social code, operated with Old Testament severity by its small-minded human agents. Not God-made, but man-made rules apply.

The 'Effi komm' telegram eventually signals the triumph of natural feelings over rigid adherence to abstract principle. Briest puts society to the test at the same time: 'Die "Gesellschaft", wenn sie nur will, kann auch ein Auge zudrücken' (p.277).

The novel closes on no note of reconciliation between individual and society. Effi's final attitude is one of fatalistic resignation. She acknowledges that she turned the blame on Innstetten ('da hab' ich ... den Spieß umgekehrt', p.294), in her desperation over Annie, and finds a restricted happiness ('das kleine Glück') by withdrawing to a private world, on which society as such does not impinge. Her final pronouncement accepts the superiority of society's norms, and finds ultimate peace only in death. She is content to leave life's 'Tafel' early, before the feast is over, for there is little remaining that invites delay (p.293). She ends her life in total renunciation. She asserts the rightness of Innstetten's conduct, and sees herself as a social failure.

> Laß ihn das wissen, daß ich in dieser Überzeugung gestorben bin. Es wird ihn trösten, aufrichten, vielleicht versöhnen. Denn er hatte viel Gutes in seiner Natur und war so edel, wie jemand sein kann, der ohne rechte Liebe ist. (p.294)

Degering identifies here a sharply felt conflict between social conformism and humanity, as though propriety and honourable conduct were at inescapable variance with *Liebe* (*2*, p.71); while Richter (*12*, p.160) sees Fontane's work as being halfway to a *Bildungsroman*. With Schopenhauerian resignation Effi transcends her own suffering through sympathy for Innstetten: no longer self-concern but concern for others leads to a degree of serenity in the final months of life at Hohen-Cremmen.

At the end of Fontane's novel the sufferers and losers are many, and the question of guilt and responsibility cannot, in the final resort, be resolved. Frau von Briest's closing words make a fitting conclusion: many people must be accounted responsible, and circumstance too. Of Effi's own individual guilt no word is spoken. But of Effi's value and desirability as a person Fontane had no doubts; above all, he stressed her quality of naturalness, a feature of many of his preferred heroines:

> Der natürliche Mensch will leben, will weder fromm noch keusch noch sittlich sein, lauter Kunstprodukte von einem gewissen, aber immer zweifelhaft bleibenden Wert, weil es an Echtheit und Natürlichkeit fehlt. Dies Natürliche hat es mir seit lange angetan, ich lege nur *da*rauf Gewicht, fühle mich nur *da*durch angezogen, und dies ist wohl der Grund, warum meine Frauengestalten alle einen Knacks weghaben. Gerade dadurch sind sie mir lieb, ich verliebe mich in sie, nicht um ihrer Tugenden, sondern um ihrer Menschlichkeiten, d.h. um ihrer Schwächen und Sünden willen. (letter of 10 October 1895)

To be human is to be prone to mortal imperfections; to deny them is spiritual blindness; to condemn them may be hypocrisy; and to punish them is to come close to tyranny. Society also has its needs, however, and Fontane's comprehension of them is part of the fundamental challenge that issues from his work.

3. Portrait of a Society

It is on the social commentary of Fontane's art that most critics have focussed their attention, Müller-Seidel for instance conceiving of his novels collectively in terms of a *Soziale Romankunst in Deutschland* (8). That the seeking for truth-to-life was an overriding concern of Fontane is borne out by his statement of 14 February 1875 in a review for the *Vossische Zeitung*: 'Das wird der beste Roman sein, dessen Gestalten sich in die Gestalten des wirklichen Lebens einreihen, so daß wir in Erinnerung an eine bestimmte Lebensepoche nicht mehr wissen, ob es gelebte oder gelesene Figuren waren ...'. Precision and accuracy are his aim, rather than criticism and condemnation: Fontane was in no sense a revolutionary, nor even a reformer. His declared purpose is to stimulate the reader's own critical self-awareness: 'schon viel gewonnen, wenn die moderne Menschheit zur Einsicht kommt; wenn sie sich im Spiegel sieht und einen Schreck kriegt' (letter of 27 May 1891). Only from the individual's stance can any change be generated, and 'insight' is the necessary prerequisite. In her own limited way, Frau von Briest arrives at this point in her closing words.

Fontane's angle of approach is nonetheless far from dispassionate. The total subjugation of the individual to society was most offensive to him, and he saw it at its worst in the polite social world of late nineteenth-century Prussia. Above all, he makes society's attitude to its female members a touchstone by which to evaluate it. In almost every case, they emerge as second-class citizens. Effi knows and accepts instantly the consequences of Innstetten's discovery of her deception: loss of all her possessions and of all protection in life. How, and even whether, she will survive, seems of the utmost unconcern to others — above all Innstetten, despite his claim that he still loves her and is capable of forgiveness.

The degree of discretion and personal freedom enjoyed by

Effi after her marriage is severely limited. Her position as wife to the local *Landrat* dictates the whole pattern of her life. There are few houses in Kessin where she may visit: the clergyman, the doctor, the chemist, the harbourmaster and the depressive Frau Crampas are socially 'safe', but few others 'belong'. If concern for her husband's reputation governs Effi's private life, his career dictates her public one. The pattern of the social year is immutable: it falls into two distinct phases, a social season and a close season. At the start of winter, the social season requires them first of all to make their *Stadtbesuche* to the few eligible houses of the town, and when these are completed, the rural aristocracy must receive its due. A fortnight is devoted exclusively to journeys to the outlying estates, a whole day consumed by each visit.

Social visiting need not, by nature, be dreary and depressing; but the *Landadel*, by and large, have precious little to recommend them. Petty-minded, jealous, parochial and terrified of new ideas, they exhaust not only Effi but Innstetten too. Fontane deals with them in one highly dismissive paragraph:

> Der Eindruck, den Effi empfing, war überall derselbe: mittelmäßige Menschen, von meist zweifelhafter Liebenswürdigkeit, die, während sie vorgaben, über Bismarck und die Kronprinzessin zu sprechen, eigentlich nur Effis Toilette musterten, die von einigen als zu prätentiös für eine so jugendliche Dame, von andern als zu wenig dezent für eine Dame von gesellschaftlicher Stellung befunden wurde. Man merke doch an allem die Berliner Schule ... (p.65)

And if it is not Effi's clothes and manner that are attacked, it is her lack of traditional religious fervour, which clearly marks her out for Sidonie von Grasenabb as an atheist (p.65). While the womenfolk demolish the young and vivacious Effi, Innstetten is bogged down in a sterile conversation with the menfolk about politics and local farming problems. He is 'klug genug ..., auf solche Philistereien anscheinend ernsthaft einzugehen' (p.66).

Pretence is the essential here.

The political allegiances and intellectual qualities of this landed gentry are displayed by Fontane in the set-piece account of the party that takes place in the house of Oberförster Ring just after Christmas, where all the paraphernalia of their private obsessions are trotted out. Ring, the very essence of hospitality, is secretly scorned by certain of the visiting gentry, for he has been promoted, as it were, from the ranks; and, much worse, his mother was a washerwoman in Köslin (p.153). Meanwhile, Sidonie von Grasenabb reminds the clergyman of the church's duty to see to the preservation of the established order in society (p.154): and she is apprehensive that Ring is becoming ostentatious in his life-style — much beyond his true station.

At Hohen-Cremmen, in the heartland of old Prussia, pressures are less acute and pretensions fewer. Herr von Briest is content to be a successful landowner, proud of his ancestry yet without vanity, and has rejected political involvement (beyond the perfunctory membership of the local council, as *Ritterschaftsrat*) in favour of a comfortable, if limited life-style. His unconcern over challenging issues and his parochialism are well reflected in his favourite dictum: 'Das ist ein zu weites Feld'. The Briests are, as Pascal observes (*9*, p.202), oblivious of intellectual and moral problems, safe in their rural seclusion: delightful people, but unequal to the challenge of the new. Pastor Niemeyer represents a church with a similar quietist philosophy, happy to play tutor to the younger generation and write verses for social occasions, but little moved by weighty issues: a man 'contained' by his parish and his duties to his patron.

Further away from the centre, in Hinterpommern where Kessin lies, society has not settled into such harmonious balance. Historical and political factors have militated against this: the population is a mixed one; the Prussian element is mostly a veneer superimposed on a basically Slav substratum, product of the Prussian *Drang nach Osten* of earlier centuries. Kessin itself is a veritable melting-pot of nationalities, drawn there by its maritime trade. Such contrasts are productive of suspicion, social climbing and exploitation. Innstetten, as a politician, must be constantly alert to these realities. We notice how he pays flattering attention to Golchowski, a Pole of aristocratic extraction, in the service of the Prussian state, and thus an indirect controlling influence on the indigent population. Innstetten is quick to introduce Effi to him: he is affable to all about him indeed, and makes a point of asking a bystander to light his cigar. Such gestures win votes. At times local acts of sabotage are suspected, and Innstetten must go to investigate: his plans to go riding with Effi are frustrated when three farms are burnt down in the vicinity. The tensions that build up in Innstetten have to be soothed by Effi's playing of Wagner, then at the height of fashion (p.103); and Bismarck looms in the background as a reminder of power political complexities. He plays no active part in the novel, but his presence is felt in all kinds of ways: even the *Gasthaus* where Effi and Innstetten have lunch bears his name. It is ultimately on him that Innstetten depends (p.365), and his all-pervasive presence gives the novel the quality of a *Zeitroman* (p.358).

The life-style of Innstetten and his wife becomes easier and more sophisticated with their arrival in the capital. They do the accepted things. They live in a highly desirable residential quarter, and there are ample material rewards for membership of this inner circle: lunch at Hiller's restaurant, one of Berlin's foremost establishments, social calls on the polite world and receptions at home. Here too there is a visiting season, which runs from March to early May, after which one can relax and be oneself at home or go for pleasant afternoon walks (p.207). In the summer, there is a month's leave, with servants to take care of house and family, while parents tour. Little wonder that Effi can tell her mother how much happier she is with Innstetten now. Her social ambitions are being realised just as her mother predicted on the day of her engagement. Two years' 'correct' behaviour brings the approval of the Empress: Effi joins the ranks of her ladies of honour (p.222) and is graciously addressed by the Emperor himself. And when she is indisposed, three weeks of spa life at Schwalbach, followed by a further three at Bad Ems are the automatic recommendation of Dr. Rummschüttel (p.223).

So pleasant, civilised and sophisticated an existence depends, however, on total identification with the accepted code. For those who place so much as one foot outside this charmed circle, the image is transformed and a fearsome vengeance is visited upon the transgressor. Effi's revealed adultery segregates her totally from her social contacts. She must not only now resort to a discreet and withdrawn mode of life, but is even prevented from joining in charitable or cultural activities and so loses all prospects of making a meaningful life for herself.

It is a rigid and long-established code that operates, and Innstetten does not easily reconcile himself to its rule. Fontane presents his analysis in the closing chapters of his work, where Innstetten's initial hesitations are overcome by sober reflections and the consciousness that this society constitutes a cohesive force: 'Man ist nicht bloß ein einzelner Mensch, man gehört einem Ganzen an, und auf das Ganze haben wir beständig Rücksicht zu nehmen, wir sind durchaus abhängig von ihm' (p.235). He conceives of society as an organisation of individuals operating together according to a mutually accepted code; rejection of this code would invite social disintegration. But the ideal has faded and in place of consensus a tyrannical force has evolved which makes captives of its members: 'jenes ... uns tyrannisierende Gesellschafts-Etwas' (p.236). It takes no account of human emotions or mitigating circumstance: 'das fragt nicht nach Charme und nicht nach Liebe und nicht nach Verjährung. Ich habe keine Wahl. Ich muß'. The surrender of his free will is the price Innstetten pays in order to continue to belong.

The Hegelian view of society had posited a structure in which individual need was subordinate to the needs of the state, its corporate identity subsuming the individual identities of its citizens, giving collective expression to their will. This overriding force nevertheless constituted a guarantee of the individual's material security, creating the conditions for his private happiness. Effi and Innstetten, however, experience society's collective being as a hostile and inhibiting force, and the Hegelian ideal is rejected by Fontane. In this he joins forces with a number of writers of his time.

Degering (*2*, p.72) praises Fontane's realism in the avoidance of a trivialised ending. None of the characters experiences true satisfaction with life: and all must find an accommodation with society based on resignation and renunciation. Both Effi and Innstetten come to this realisation, giving the novel some quality of the *Bildungsroman*, though in a negative sense (see *2*, p.67). Most of the characters carry symbolic incapacities as they struggle for happiness (Gieshübler's hunchback, Roswitha's imprinted memory of the fire-iron, Crampas' injured arm) and any happiness they do achieve is a very private and severely limited one — Herr von Briest's glass of red wine, Marietta Trippelli's 'magic hours', Gieshübler's and Wüllersdorf's aesthetic interests.

The crux of this debate is constituted by the conversation between Innstetten and Wüllersdorf after the former's promotion. 'Es quält mich seit Jahr und Tag schon, und ich möchte aus dieser ganzen Geschichte heraus; nichts gefällt mir mehr ... Mein Leben ist verpfuscht' (p.287), complains Innstetten. His suggested flight into a 'Robinsonade' is rejected by Wüllersdorf, who instead proposes the military-sounding course of 'Einfach hierbleiben und Resignation üben ... In der Bresche stehen und aushalten, bis man fällt' (p.288). Stoical fortitude, backed by the little pleasures in life, treasured for their own sake: the violets flowering in spring, little girls skipping: or reflection on the greater suffering of others in the call of duty — like the late Kaiser Friedrich who has recently died of cancer. Distraction after work can be found at the ballet; followed by a visit to Siechen's famous *Bierrestaurant* in the Behrenstraße, where three good measures of ale do the trick (p.289).

Such sources of relief are referred to as 'Hilfskonstruktionen' ('props') by Wüllersdorf: with such scaffolding he buttresses his life. (The expression, we note, was coined by a builder.) Wüllersdorf departs for a walk along the canal, to be followed by a convivial glass of wine, over which some lively gossip will be exchanged: 'Dreiviertel stimmt nicht, aber wenn es nur witzig ist, krittelt man nicht lange dran herum und hört dankbar zu' (p.289). A society of 'hollow men' is conjectured: Fontane sees acutely the channelling of citizen and individual into differentiated spheres, suggesting that total divorce of individual human qualities and participation in public affairs which lay at the very heart of the society of his day.

The class that lived in accordance with this convention was, as Pascal says (*9*, p.206), 'moribund, even to the point of being incapable of understanding the causes of its failure'.

4. *Marietta Trippelli and the Limits of Independence*

Social forces are all-compelling, it would appear. Certain figures in the story seem nevertheless to constitute exceptions to this condition. Chief among them is the singer, Marietta Trippelli. Fontane here explores a thematic area that is closely associated with the question of the artist and his place in society. Critics have largely neglected to comment on this dimension of the novel.

Fontane has already introduced Fräulein Trippelli's father before she makes her entrance. He was the self-willed clergyman, now deceased, who presided at the wedding of Captain Thomsen's vanished niece (or granddaughter) and who was at odds with Kessin's inhabitants over the Chinaman's burial. His widow still lives in Kessin. Her daughter, Marie, had seen only one way of emancipating herself from her incarceration in Kessin society: she embarked on a musical career, which was to open up for her much wider prospects than would otherwise be available to a woman in her position. That her emancipation has been achieved becomes clear on the occasion of the musical soirée at Gieshübler's.

Much of her achievement is the result of the support and guidance of Gieshübler. It was he who sent her off to Paris to be trained, possibly out of a sense of obligation to his friend, her deceased father. Here she has studied for several years under the mezzo-soprano Viardot (Pauline Viardot-Garcia, one of the foremost singers and teachers of the time). In Paris she also became acquainted with the Russian Prince Kotschukoff, who took her under his wing and induced her to italianise, i.e. 'liberate', her name. Now an accomplished singer, she performs in the great European and American cities. En route from Paris to St. Petersburg, where she will give performances for several weeks, she is paying the briefest of visits to native regions to see her mother and her mentor, Gieshübler.

The reception at Gieshübler's illustrates most compellingly the power to dominate on social occasions which Marietta has acquired: it is a self-assertiveness which quite frightens her convention-ridden mother. Her self-confidence is expressed both in her behaviour and in the mode of her speech, and it impresses the young and insecure Effi more than anyone else present. There is a positiveness about her actions and a dismissiveness in the treatment of unwelcome views that are almost overbearing, and Gieshübler gently apologises for her, acknowledging his responsibility as host. Yet all is carried off with such panache that it is impossible to feel offended. Whatever does not suit her musical taste is contemptuously tossed aside and its advocates diminished to the status of *ignoranti*; all this conducted with a verve, a passion and a wit which are utterly compelling (p.92).

It is a superb scene, in which Marietta the artist is always to the fore. She warms to the occasion, expands to the full display of her considerable abilities, lives in the music as her very own element, free of constraint, and gratefully drinks in the plaudits of her listeners: she is conscious of being quite the equal of Effi (p.90).

What is the reality behind this impressive façade? Has Marietta really emancipated herself from society's constraints? And if so, at what cost? A close reading of Fontane's work reveals the price that has to be paid. Long journeys, often with considerable discomfort; no permanent home, but constant travel and dependence on the hospitality of others. She has, she tells them, learnt to sleep in a railway carriage, in all possible positions; but what really concerns her is the durability of her fame: 'was wir regelmäßig brauchen, heißt Beifall und hohe Preise' (p.94). The artist's life is precarious and his deliberate disconnection of himself from social bonds is a freedom that is bought at a price.

In the last resort the artist depends on society and must woo its support through his talents. It will give him short shrift when these fail. Innstetten's characteristically *moral* reference to the dangers of too much public self-exposure is interpreted in a different sense by her: 'Ja, beständig gefährdet; am meisten die

Stimme' (p.96). Technical, not ethical, concerns beset her: circumstance, not morality.

The telegram to Effi which proclaims Marietta's arrival in St. Petersburg does not fool Innstetten, for all its make-believe excitement and French formulation. It is intended to impress — part of the *Komödie* which she constantly enacts: 'Alles berechnet für dort und für hier, für Kotschukoff und für Gieshübler. Gieshübler wird wohl eine Stiftung machen, vielleicht auch bloß ein Legat für die Trippelli' (p.96). Her talents will not last for ever; and a legacy from Gieshübler would be a great reassurance later in life. We hear subsequently that Marietta is engaged in an active correspondence with Gieshübler over her financial situation: she is seeking fresh support from him, though already in his debt. The profligate artist theme is thus gently sounded.

At table, Effi contrasts her own subjective approach to the world with the detached confidence of her artistic neighbour:

> Ich bin so leicht Eindrücken hingegeben, und wenn ich die kleinste Gespenstergeschichte höre, so zittere ich und kann mich kaum wieder zurechtfinden. Und Sie tragen das so mächtig und erschütternd vor und sind selbst ganz heiter und guter Dinge. (p.93)

'Ja, meine gnädigste Frau, das ist in der Kunst nicht anders', is the reply, and with it the age-old contrast of *Natur* and *Kunst* is adumbrated by Fontane. Where Marietta exemplifies the abstracted and rarefied world of art, Effi stands for that of nature.

However, it is in her art alone that Marietta can find escape, and that is a non-enduring prerogative: for the rest of the time she must conform. She admits that her private agnosticism is a privilege that is unacceptable, indeed unviable, at the social level. In fact, she sides with the public view of the Chinaman's ineligibility for Christian burial, and asserts that she would always be the first to insist on social conformity: 'Staatlich höre der Spaß auf' (p.95). Like Crampas, she delights in challenging society privately, while espousing its conventions in public.

(Crampas, we note, declines to desert his institutional marriage when invited to do so by Effi, thus refusing a public commitment to his private liberty-taking (see 2, p.45).

Two other figures suggest themselves for consideration as having achieved a position from which they can afford to ignore society's dictates: Alonzo Gieshübler and Geheimrat Rummschüttel. Gieshübler seems to have been singled out by fate for an 'outsider' role in life. A hunchback, short-sighted, and it would seem totally non-athletic, this rather pathetic bachelor lives alone and detached. '... ich bin eigentlich nie jung gewesen', he tells Effi (p.63), 'Personen meines Schlages sind nie jung'. He declines to use his academic title, in deference to those who are by profession 'real' doctors (p.51). His very name is indicative of a confusion of identities, Alonzo ('ein Preziosaname', says Effi (p.64)) deriving from his mother, a Spanish sea-captain's daughter whom his father, an apothecary of old Pomeranian stock, had married in Kessin. A combination of romantic imagination and humble servitude is the outcome.

Consolation and contentment are found by him in the cultivation of the mind, in the world of music, cuisine and books. He is an assiduous newspaper reader, stands 'an der Spitze des Journalzirkels' (p.102), and delights in marking any interesting passages and sending them over to the *Landrathaus*. A potential hermit, he is a challenge to nobody; he would appear therefore to be in a position to lead his life as he chooses, disregarding the requirements of society. Yet that is not his chosen course. Commitment to life is strong in him, and he plays an active part in imbuing the society of Kessin with a sense of purpose. '... er ist unsere beste Nummer hier, Schöngeist und Original und vor allem Seele von Mensch, was doch immer die Hauptsache bleibt', is Innstetten's introduction of him (p.51). He is a committee member of the Kessin *Ressource* (social club) and a prime mover in the production of the play *Ein Schritt vom Wege* in which Effi appears. We have already noted his generous support of the career of Marietta Trippelli. A free-thinker who goes his own way in matters of religion, he nevertheless is a firm upholder of tradition and good-neighbourliness; Christmas is the time for the sending of gifts to others — usually accompanied by a specially composed dedication — and he is particularly attentive to Effi, sending her little presents, invitations and gifts of flowers, as though endeavouring to make good the neglect of these gestures by Innstetten. He is utterly shattered when he hears of Effi's infidelity and the duel. Social commitment is, even in his case, the principle by which one must live. The alternative is total and ineffectual isolation. He is clearly intended by Fontane as one of the few positive figures in his book, and it is perhaps no accident that his creator has made an apothecary of him.

Dr. Rummschüttel is the only person of social standing to maintain any links with Effi after her separation from Innstetten. Indeed, he actually chooses to visit her, totally disregarding her social ignominy. Rummschüttel's strength lies in his professional skills and the knowledge that society has need of them: at his advanced age and with his accumulated expertise he can afford the luxury of free choice. Yet things have not always stood that way. As a younger man, he had to establish his name by paying close attention to the whims and susceptibilities of the polite world. His clientele grew as his appeal, especially for the ladies, grew. Frau von Briest, having been flatteringly attended by him in her youth, recommends him to Effi twenty years later, and his resourcefulness and tact with her little deception of Innstetten leads to his becoming their *Hausarzt* in Berlin. Like the artist, the professional man can, on the strength of his skills, at times disregard the constraints of society. But he must first have gained its trust and admiration. Rummschüttel's licence to visit the disgraced Effi implies a humanitarian concern for her well-being which gives him the right to inform her parents of the deterioration in her condition and to remind them of their own obligation towards their daughter. Even in old age, he is conscious of likely shortcomings in his career, though without obsessive self-accusation. (Bance (*1*, p.54) makes the interesting observation that he is approximately the same age as Fontane at the time of writing *Effi Briest*.) Self-irony manifests itself as, looking out of Effi's window at the cemetery, he asks himself the question: 'könnten hier nicht vielleicht einige weniger liegen?' (p.259). Integrity and humanity constitute the basis on

which Rummschüttel is able, on occasion, to cock a snook at
social convention. An independent figure, but by no means a
social outsider.

Fontane suggests a mutual obligation of individual and
society, which grants the individual the opportunity to show the
quality of his spirit; it is on this that the collective quality of
society itself depends. As a member of his society, Innstetten is
conscious that he has assumed responsibilities and duties as well
as prerogatives:

> Man ist nicht bloß ein einzelner Mensch, man gehört einem
> Ganzen an, und auf das Ganze haben wir beständig
> Rücksicht zu nehmen, wir sind durchaus abhängig von
> ihm. (p.235)

Innstetten's words acknowledge this relationship, but his
attitude is unduly subservient. An active commitment is needed,
not a passive one; and all such activity must be conditioned by
charity and understanding: without 'rechte Liebe' society
remains inadequate.

5. The 'Spuk'

Of all the symbolic devices used in Fontane's work, none is so pervasively and consistently employed as the ghost of Captain Thomsen's erstwhile Chinese servant. Fontane takes up the motif from the 'Gothic' or trivial novel, but he invests it with an infinitely higher poetic quality. It operates to highlight the thought-processes and motives of a number of characters, chief among them Effi herself.

That Fontane himself considered this 'Spuk' to be an important element in the novel is indicated in a letter to Joseph Widmann of 19 November 1895:

> erstlich ist dieser Spuk ... an und für sich interessant, und zweitens ... steht die Sache nicht zum Spaß da, sondern ist ein Drehpunkt für die ganze Geschichte.

Critics have only reluctantly followed up Fontane's lead: as recently as 1964, J.P. Stern dismissed the 'Spuk' as 'a blemish ..., a piece of bric-à-brac left over from Poetic Realism' (*16*, p.319). Most commentators have been content to take it purely at face value.

Turning first to its 'interesting' quality, we find an intriguing history which fascinates the imaginative Effi. It is one reflection among many of the strange society which has gathered in Kessin from all over the globe. Retiring from the business of shipping rice between Shanghai and Singapore, the Danish Captain Thomsen settled in Kessin and there bought the house where Effi and Innstetten now live. The crocodile, the shark and the model ship that hang in the hall came with him; so also did a young woman about twenty years of age who was variously believed to be his niece or granddaughter; and also, of course, the Chinese servant. The whole history of the Thomsen household is shrouded in uncertainties, especially the episode of the young woman's disappearance from her wedding reception and the death fourteen days later of the Chinaman. Innstetten himself seems ignorant of the circumstances, and Effi's attempts to elicit the facts from Johanna and Frau Kruse are totally unproductive. Only the Chinaman's grave, barred from sanctified ground, provides tangible evidence of the whole episode.

The aura of mysteriousness is compounded by the fact that the ill-fated wedding was celebrated by Pastor Trippel, a clergyman from Berlin, who was, as an 'outsider', distrusted by many in Kessin's society and incurred so much hostility by his charitable attitude to the subsequent question of the Chinaman's burial, that he himself died of stress shortly afterwards. Among the guests at the wedding were the eccentric Gieshübler, whose religious beliefs were suspect in the town, and the miller Utpatel, a follower of the free-thinking conventicle movement. Fontane suggests that here were a number of figures who suffered at the hands of a moralistically hidebound society. The Chinaman has been consigned by society to the role of an unedifying and admonitory figure from the past. His grave stands abandoned and unheeded at the edge of the town, while his memory is perpetuated by naive devices like the cut-out figure pasted on the arm of a chair in the abandoned attic room where the wedding reception took place. Johanna, the rigid conformist, can speak in quite normal tones about him: he represents no challenge to her.

When Effi first hears of the Chinaman the incident is briefly related, but already demonstrates her proclivity for romanticising or demonising events (at school, her strongest subject was mythology, she tells her daughter (p.273)). Effi, when she arrives in Kessin, hopes to find 'Allerlei Exotisches ... Eine ganz neue Welt ... vielleicht einen Neger oder einen Türken, oder vielleicht sogar einen Chinesen' (p.45). Innstetten replies that her hopes are to be fulfilled: a Chinaman lies buried in a little grave not far from the churchyard, and if she is not too fearful he will show it to her. Its 'schauerlich' aspects both attract and repel Effi, who forebodingly decides not to hear more about it at present:

ich habe dann immer gleich Visionen und Träume und
möchte doch nicht, wenn ich diese Nacht hoffentlich gut
schlafe, gleich einen Chinesen an mein Bett treten sehen.
(p.46)

As yet, Effi knows nothing of the Chinaman's history, but her
fertile imagination is already at work: 'Ein Chinese, find' ich,
hat immer was Gruseliges' (p.46). The unusual and exotic have
been represented to her in threatening terms at Hohen-
Cremmen.

It is not until some days later that she hears the history of the
Thomsen house and its Chinese servant. In the meantime her
sleep has really been disturbed, by the sound of curtains trailing
over the floor of the room above her — sounding in her
imagination like long clothes or satin shoes. Her maid, Johanna,
is greatly intrigued to observe the anxious reactions of her new
mistress — who receives no explanation why the offending
curtains have not been shortened (p.54).

A crucial experience in the Chinaman's life was the dance, a
high point in his years of hopeless longing. In his purgatorial
existence, he seems now condemned to re-enact this moment:
time has stood still for him. He becomes an augury of Effi's own
fate, as she too is trapped in what she comes to see as a hopeless
dilemma. And the theme of dance fits well with Effi's known
character and uncertain anchorage in practical affairs. Far from
home, among unloving and unsympathetic people, she is almost
as much an outcast as he was. Like the Chinaman, whose
feelings were killed off by social taboos, Effi too will give up
hope and wither.

As yet, however, Effi knows nothing of the Chinaman's
history. A tour of the house the next day brings the encounter
with the cut-out picture, and Innstetten himself seems surprised
by it. He supposes it to have been put there by Johanna or
Christel, but devotes more attention to it than Effi considers
normal. It is just possible that Johanna placed it there after that
morning's conversation with Effi. Throughout the story she
shows herself a firm admirer of Innstetten and after the move to
Berlin takes the picture with her in her purse, possibly as a

warning to Effi, for whose spontaneous naturalness she appears to have a rigorous distrust. A further reference by Johanna to the Chinaman had occurred when she warned Effi, during her pregnancy, that any new arrival in the Landrathaus was liable to summon the ghostly figure (p.100). The suggestion is that the introduction of any new way of life into the house will conjure up the spirit, with implied destabilising effects. Johanna seems to be exploiting the tradition as a control mechanism over her mistress.

Effi's arrival in Kessin confronts her with considerable challenges, not least that of Innstetten's own stern character. Her hypersensitive nature impels her to transfer her fears into some paranormal force on the first occasion when she is left alone in the Landrathaus. The facts are deliberately left unspecific by Fontane. There are indications that a mysterious power is operating, in the manner in which Rollo behaves, barking and dashing into the room and laying himself protectively beside Effi's bed: though the explanation could be that Rollo, having sensed some acute distress in his mistress, is simply prompted to come to her aid. Certainly Effi has built up a deep state of anxiety in herself. Denied the company of social equals and finding no response from the servants, especially the fantasy-engrossed Frau Kruse whose head is full of stories like that of the Chinaman, to the detriment of her duties (p.175), Effi has sought relief by recalling scenes from her childhood, then playing the piano and finally reading. None of these has lifted her out of her melancholia, and the page at which she opens the book unhappily recounts the story of the 'weiße Frau', a ghost said to haunt Schloß Eremitage, near Bayreuth, and to have alarmed Napoleon as he slept there — very much the experience Effi shortly afterwards undergoes, and which she had already jestingly predicted to Innstetten on the day of their arrival in Kessin.

Effi, overcome by a sense of inadequacy and ineffectuality, now prepares for bed. The event which jolts her from her sleep bears marked similarities to a nightmare: a sudden frightened awakening, accompanied by a desire to cry out which is yet frustrated by fear. There is a tradition of nightmares in her family, as she tells Johanna: 'Alpdruck ist in unserer Familie, mein Papa hat es auch und ängstigt uns damit' (p.75). Johanna dismisses it as a bad dream and next morning reports the event to Innstetten in total detachment, as though to criticise her mistress's overwrought behaviour.

Innstetten is ambivalent in his reaction: one can choose to believe in ghosts, or not to believe, and he finds it preferable not to believe and implies that he expects Effi to make the same choice. Having pointed out the political inadvisability of leaving their house simply because it was possibly haunted and his wife was afraid, an argument in which Effi acquiesces, Innstetten takes matters a step too far and shows gross lack of consideration for her feelings. He is surprised to see a Briest behave in so abject a way, so unbecoming in an aristocrat: 'Das ist ja, wie wenn du aus einem kleinen Bürgerhause stammtest' (p.80). For him, the Chinaman represents an additional attribute of the house in which he lives — just as many noblemen's houses have their resident ghost: a status symbol pure and simple. 'Spuk ist ein Vorzug, wie Stammbaum und dergleichen, und ich kenne Familien, die sich ebensogern ihr Wappen nehmen ließen als ihre "weiße Frau", die natürlich auch eine schwarze sein kann' (p.80). This intellectualised jesting (a feature of several of Fontane's 'flawed' husbands) is foreign to Effi's nature and shows how casually he views her genuine anxieties.

Effi is even able to show him the contradictoriness of his attitude: for, while seemingly dismissing the ghost as a figment of her imagination, he is at the same time enjoying its ownership and requiring a similar 'adligen Spukstolz' of Effi (p.80). She claims the Briests to be free of such superstitious nonsense by the quality of their minds. Effi attempts to combat the impact of Innstetten's priorities, but has to do so on his terms, which drive her own subjectivity underground. For Avery (*18*, p.34) the Chinaman represents Fontane's criticism of a society that shapes Effi's consciousness and makes her its victim by debasing her vitality to fear and self-doubt.

The 'Spuk' can also be understood as an embodiment of Effi's approach to the marital experience. Fascination with the new and profound dimension to her existence which she is entering combines with a fear of the unexplored; tensions which Innstetten fails to resolve through his lack of passion and devotion — for he is 'ohne rechte Liebe'. It is only after the birth of her child, and then her affair with Crampas, that Effi seems to Innstetten a fully matured woman (p.179): by then, the ghost of the Chinaman is no more a spectre that haunts her.

Up to the point of Effi's nightmare, the details of the Chinaman's history have not been revealed to her. It is Effi herself who finally insists on hearing them during the sleigh-ride the following day.

> Solang ich es nicht weiß, bin ich, trotz aller guten Vorsätze, doch immer ein Opfer meiner Vorstellungen. Erzähle mir das Wirkliche. Die Wirklichkeit kann mich nicht so quälen wie meine Phantasie. (p.84)

Effi's seeking to bring the tradition within social norms is clear, and once in possession of the facts, she associates herself with the townsfolk's condemnation of the unconventional Pastor Trippel and re-asserts her belief in 'Ordnung' and her desire to further Innstetten's prospects and their joint social advancement. She characterises her fears as childish and reaffirms her affection for Innstetten (p.82). The struggle between social ambition and private self-indulgence is becoming sharper.

Effi's deeper engrossment with the exotic and unusual leads her now to turn away from Hohen-Cremmen and to prefer 'das Aparte' which Kessin offers in such figures as the ghostly Chinaman. Innstetten feels compelled to warn her: 'Spuk, dazu kann man sich stellen, wie man will. Aber hüte dich vor dem Aparten oder was man so das Aparte nennt. Was dir so verlockend erscheint, … das bezahlt man in der Regel mit seinem Glück' (p.87). 'Das Aparte' represents an assertion of subjective needs. It need not constitute a threat to fortune and happiness; indeed, it may serve a salutary function in this hidebound society. Innstetten, rigidly self-disciplined himself, fails to comprehend the need for safety valves which enable society to deal with suppressed sexuality, vitality and idealisms. But Effi's conception of 'das Aparte' is here moving away from earlier associations with the elegant and chic to more subjective and disintegrative realms. Her conversation that evening with Marietta Trippelli on the subject of ghost ballads illustrates her continuing struggle to come to terms with her irrational self.

The regular, uneventful routine which precedes the birth of her child then renders life so monotonous that she jestingly wishes for the excitement of a modified return of the 'Spuk' (p.104), whose power she hopes she has exorcised through the recruitment of the devout Roswitha.

The figure of the Chinaman is given more sinister force by Crampas, who, while disbelieving the tradition himself, exploits it as a means of estranging husband and wife, feeding the strain of pleasure-seeking rebellion that is latent in Effi and undermining that part of her which believes in 'Ordnung' and ambitious commitment to duty. Crampas recalls moments from their military service when Innstetten had told ghost stories to his colleagues, only to break the tension suddenly, as though mocking their credulity and addiction to trivial escapism (p.131). Bance (*1*, p.58) suggests that Innstetten's dismissal of ghosts is one more expression of his fear of sexuality and hidden desires. Such autocratic qualities in a man made him more impressive to his seniors, suggests Crampas, and were cultivated as an aid to promotion. Then follows the statement about Innstetten's educative proclivities, and the suggestion that he is exploiting the supernatural once more, this time to control Effi's fondness for the trivial. Although she tries to dismiss this hateful thought, she never quite overcomes the resentment that it generates (p.134), and she hears Crampas' words behind the advice spoken by Innstetten: 'Unbefangenheit ist immer das beste, und natürlich das allerbeste ist Charakter und Festigkeit und, wenn ich solch steifleinenes Wort brauchen darf, eine reine Seele' (p.147). 'Ja gewiß', replies Effi, 'Aber nun sprich nicht mehr, und noch dazu lauter Dinge, die mich nicht recht froh machen können. Weißt du, mir ist, als hörte ich oben das Tanzen. Sonderbar, daß es immer wieder kommt. Ich dachte, du hättest mit dem allen nur so gespaßt'. Effi's half-hearted cry for understanding and help cannot make itself heard against the puritanical certainty of Innstetten's own convictions.

Effi's surrender to Crampas marks a further stage in her understanding of the 'Spuk'. Now she acknowledges its existence no longer as a chimera, but as a personal spectre, the embodiment of her own guilty aberration. (The parallelism with the earlier apparition scene is striking.)

> Einmal trat sie spät abends vor den Spiegel in ihrer Schlafstube; die Lichter und Schatten flogen hin und her, und Rollo schlug draußen an, und im selben Augenblicke war es ihr, als sähe ihr wer über die Schulter. Aber sie besann sich rasch. "Ich weiß schon, was es ist; es war nicht *der*", und sie wies mit dem Finger nach dem Spukzimmer oben. "Es war was anderes ... mein Gewissen ... Effi, du bist verloren'''. (p.169)

The Chinaman subsequently represents for Effi a reminder of her unhappy experience of Kessin. She is disturbed when Johanna brings with her to Berlin the little figure from the chair, but declines Innstetten's proposal that she should instruct Johanna to get rid of it, for she knows that the real threat to her happiness lies in her conscience. (We note again Innstetten's proclivity for placing on Effi the burden of removing the 'Spuk'.) Effi prefers to ask Roswitha for a 'Heiligenschein' to help protect her from evil forces.

Increasingly Effi looks for help from such devices, signalling her sense of individual helplessness. Her initial recruitment of Roswitha was indeed presented in these terms: 'Nun wird es gehen', she told Innstetten, 'Ich fürchte mich jetzt nicht mehr' (p.114). The opposed poles of 'Spuk' and religious fervour equally elude Effi's capacities, but she hopes to play off one against the other. We note that, during her affair with Crampas, Effi dispenses with Roswitha's society, which indicates the temporary triumph of the negative principle within her. After her separation from Innstetten, however, she is glad to have Roswitha as a permanent talisman. The Chinaman no longer appears to her now; the shattering experience she has undergone has forced into the open the conflicting impulses within her. She

almost longs to exchange fantasy-haunted Kessin with the harsh
reality of the present:

> Das waren glückliche Zeiten ... weil ich das Harte des
> Lebens noch nicht kannte. Seitdem habe ich es kennen-
> gelernt. Ach, Spuk ist lange nicht das Schlimmste'. (p.262)

'Going home' to Hohen-Cremmen eases the tensions, but
cannot remove the basic conflict and produce freedom and
happiness for her. Society is now beyond her reach, a sense of
guilt still troubles her, and inner peace can only finally be found
in an acceptance of society's requirements, a gesture that is
accomplished in her dying words. The 'Spuk' within her, the
existence of uncontrolled subjective wishes, is already long since
dead and the suggested implication is that a limited degree of
happiness only becomes possible after such renunciation. In the
end, the Chinaman becomes an expression of Effi's suppressed
longing for private happiness, which is seemingly incompatible
with the social conformity (moral, religious, institutional) to
which she also aspires. The Chinaman had longings that could
not be fulfilled, except in a world that was not available to him,
and he died, apparently, of the tensions. He constitutes an *alter
ego* of Effi, and an anticipation of her fate.

The approach of Innstetten himself to 'Spuk' is an important
aspect of our investigation. In a conversation with Effi shortly
after their arrival in Berlin, as they walk through the gardens of
the supposedly haunted Charlottenburg Palace, he explains:
'Geistererscheinungen werden immer gemacht ... Spuk aber
wird nie gemacht, Spuk ist natürlich ... Es gibt so was. Nur an
das, was wir in Kessin davon hatten, glaub ich nicht recht'
(p.207). The suggestion is that a deliberately cultivated tradition
(as at Charlottenburg — or Kessin) is pure 'Spielerei' (p.61),
kept alive by trivial minds. He is angry when he suspects
Johanna of playing upon Effi's fears and tells her that the whole
business must stop (p.77). But equally, in the discussion in the
Charlottenburg gardens, Innstetten does acknowledge the
inroads of irrational forces. He is by no means as intact a person
as he wishes (and needs) to believe.

For Innstetten, 'Spuk' itself is an expression of acute disquiet, an irrational response to apprehensive emotions, and for that reason to be controlled and conquered. It represents disintegrative thoughts, to which he prefers 'Charakter und Festigkeit ... und eine reine Seele' (p.147). He would have done better to have examined with Effi the nature of her fears, for they might then have been exorcised. His would-be *Erziehung* is instead authoritarian in character, and Crampas is to that extent justified in his accusation.

Ironically, Innstetten himself becomes a victim of the uncanny, as he passes the old *Landrathaus* on his way to the duel; the questionableness of his actions towards Effi and Crampas causes ghosts of the past to haunt his conscience, and for a moment he experiences the uncanniness of the house as strongly as Effi had once done (p.241). Such ghosts however have a shorter life-span with characters as single-minded as Innstetten.

6. A Sense of Place

The opening paragraphs of Fontane's novels have often been recognised as careful stage-settings for the action which is to follow. Throughout the story a similar pattern is to be observed, providing the reader with the means of seeing the characters in context, surrounded by a substantial world that reinforces their credibility. Fontane confirms this approach in a letter of 29 October 1895: 'Daß das "Milieu" bei mir den Menschen und Dingen erst ihre Physiognomie gibt, ist gewiß richtig, auch *das*, daß ich immer sehr spät erst zur eigentlichen Geschichte komme.' One thinks naturally of Fontane's affinity with the drama and his almost life-long attempt to write a play.

Chapter 1 is essentially devoted to an evocation of life at Hohen-Cremmen, the *Heim* from which Effi never essentially escapes. The emphasis is on brightness and light, ease of living, openness, balance and naturalness. Reference is made first to the force of historical tradition: since the time of the Elector Georg Wilhelm of Prussia (1595-1640) the Briests have occupied the *Herrenhaus* at Hohen-Cremmen. Fontane then immediately moves to the present, emphasising the brightness and quiet of the setting ('fiel heller Sonnenschein auf die mittagsstille Dorfstraße', p.7). With great precision the alignment of the house with road, village church and the fields behind it is established, emphasis being laid on the rectangular lie of the side-wing and churchyard wall to the line of the main building, and on the squared pattern of the tiles along the inside of this side-wing. In contrast to the regularity of the squares is the rounded flower bed with its sundial, cannas and rhubarb stems. This sheltered interior is screened from the direct rays of the sun, yet open at the rear to the irregular contours of a pond and more distant prospects.

Nothing is really enclosed here: windows stand open, and Effi and her mother have just eaten lunch out in the garden, where they now stay to work at a tapestry for the church altar. The eye moves upwards to the spire of the church, its newly-gilded weathercock glistening in the sun, radiantly surveying the local scene.

Lest the impression given by the 'Hufeisen' configuration of house, side-wing and church wall amount to a severity of line, Fontane picks out elements that deny any sense of rigidity and are even suggestive of illogicality: the distant swing, with its seat horizontal but supports that are 'etwas schief' (like Fontane's boyhood swing at Swinemünde), a group of old and massive plane trees, half obscuring the view: Bance (*1*, p.68) suggests that the balance becomes disturbed as one looks further into the distance and an 'untidier nature looms up' — perhaps Herr von Briest's 'zu weites Feld'. Everywhere aspects of greenery and natural growth embellish and soften harsh lines and bring the world of organic growth right into the human sphere — aloes grow in tubs on the veranda, wild vines climb about the windows, the churchyard wall is cloaked with small-leaved ivy. Even the variety of the colours is stressed: the garden tiles are green and white squares, the churchyard gate is painted white, the church clock is golden, and the spools of wool of Effi and her mother lie 'bunt durcheinander' on the table, amidst dessert plates and ripe gooseberries in a majolika dish.

It is in this rural idyll that we first meet Effi, responding to its bright freshness with gymnastic exercises, a 'Tochter der Luft' (p.8). Yet, symbolically too, only a little space separates her from the stark earnestness of the adjoining graveyard: passage from one element to the other is rendered easy and swift through the medium of the little gate in the dividing wall. Fontane's fondness for adumbration is thus revealed early in the story. Riechel (*Jolles*, p.419) finds pre-Raphaelite suggestions in the scene: dressed in Mary's traditional blue and white, as in a Flemish painting, the child-woman Effi works at an altar-cloth while seated in a 'hortus conclusus', where Innstetten's arrival marks the Annunciation.

From this scene we then pass to that at Kessin and enter with Effi the portals of the *Landrathaus*, where her married life is to begin. Here, too, is brightness, as Effi first steps into the hall:

but it is a different quality of light. The illumination is provided by a concentration of wall-lamps, their brightness intensified by the highly polished tin-plate of their construction. There are five of them in the outer hall, and two other 'Astrallampen', a wedding present from Pastor Niemeyer, illuminate the inner hall. Effi is quite dazzled by this 'Fülle von Licht' (p.50). But this is a specially produced effect, artificially engineered. And the scene which they reveal departs still more from the world of nature and normality: from the ceiling hang mementoes of the past — a model ship, a stuffed shark and baby crocodile. The change in Effi's life-style is already adumbrated. The scene on the very next morning is considerably modified, with Effi's glance into the *Flur*, 'der bei der Tagesbeleuchtung viel von seinem Zauber vom Abend vorher eingebüßt hatte' (p.54). Is Effi's own disillusionment hinted at in these words?

At Hohen-Cremmen Effi scarcely seemed to inhabit the interior of the house: at Kessin she lives almost entirely indoors. And whereas Fontane provided little detail of the interior of the *Herrenhaus*, we soon become closely acquainted with the inner appearance of the *Landrathaus*. Its garden, on the other hand, hardly merits a mention: Innstetten is not a gardener, Effi informs her mother, and the garden is almost empty of plants (p.119). Order, regularity and a certain emptiness — both physical and spiritual — are the qualities that attach themselves to the Landrathaus: an impression that is reinforced by the tour of the house which is made next morning. The house even lacks a dining-room, and no entertainment seems ever to take place there (*Jolles*, p.414). Effi's late rising after her restless first night jars against this atmosphere of spartan orderliness, and she already feels intuitively 'out of her element'.

Berlin constitutes one further aspect of Effi's history. It is not the busy streets, the shops and offices that Fontane describes, but rather the world which Effi inhabits. The Keith Straße is located in one of the most desirable areas of the city. Overlooking the zoological gardens and park and fronting the Landwehrkanal, it stands in green surroundings and constitutes a peaceful retreat with delightful prospects. Effi steps on to the balcony of their new home and enjoys a prospect which symbolises her rising hopes: '... schon überall einen grünen Schimmer ... Darüber aber ein klarer blauer Himmel und eine lachende Sonne' (p.202).

The Keith Straße was, of course, a real street in Berlin and could be found on a map of the city. So also could all the other street and place names which Fontane uses. Effi arrives in Berlin at the Friedrichstraßen-Bahnhof and takes a cab that travels 'neben dem Pferdebahngleise [introduced in 1878] hin in die Dorotheenstraße hinein und auf die Schadowstraße zu, an deren nächstgelegener Ecke sich die ''Pension'' befand' (p.192). The authenticity of the novel is in part guaranteed by such exactness of detail.

The broad sweep of events around Kessin is placed into spatial context in the overall structure of the narrative by a system of key points that is established by Fontane quite early in the novel. This enables the reader to trace the movements of the characters and to see them against certain backgrounds, rather in the manner of simple stage settings. The key points set up by Fontane include *Utpatels Mühle*, the *Kirchhof*, the *Dünen* and *Strandhotel*, the Chinaman's grave, the *Plantage* and the church towers of Kroschentin and of Morgenitz and the railway station at Klein Tantow. Effi's walks, excursions with Innstetten and Crampas and assignations are all brought into relationship with these points, and no further indication is needed of her precise location. Effi's secret meetings with Crampas occur, significantly, not far from the Chinaman's grave (Fontane barely indicates the link), and the duel is fought where Effi and Crampas had picnicked.

Kessin itself is substantially depicted. In addition to the careful locating of the 'Landrathaus' in relation to the town, Fontane provides us with ample information about Kessin's inhabitants, its history and commercial life. Innstetten's account as he and Effi approach their new home constitutes a potted history and testifies to his command of local conditions. 'Das ist ja aber großartig, Geert', exclaims Effi. 'Das ist ja wie sechs Romane, damit kann man ja gar nicht fertig werden' (p.47). Yet the engrossment of Effi with all this remains at one remove: it is a world from which she is socially segregated, except on certain very precise terms.

Lesser events and minor figures can also be authenticated by such physical settings. Fontane's action is then able to unfold unimpeded by the need for descriptive pauses, and the dialogue in particular can be given free rein. Our first proper acquaintance with Major von Crampas is made on the occasion of his accompanying Effi and Innstetten to the harbour entrance. Significantly, we never meet him in his home. Their ride along the shore to the estuary and the mole is briefly recounted; the wide sweep of the river is reached, flowing out to the sea between controlling stone-laid banks, and the riders dismount to walk to the end of the mole and the open prospect. The moment for revelations has arrived, as so often in Fontane's *Landpartien*, and Crampas and Innstetten engage in a conversation which turns on the question of respect for the law and correct behaviour. It is now that Crampas produces his characteristic formulation: 'Alle Gesetzlichkeiten sind langweilig' (p.128). The natural and elemental is a fitting setting for these exchanges, particularly where it is tangibly seen breaking free from man-made restraints.

The element of time can also be represented by such physical means. Fontane presents a historical perspective of the Ring family, mostly through the medium of pictures hung on their wall, so that the reader has numerous points of reference for what follows: Ring's wife derives from a rich Danzig corn merchant's family, and most of the ornate and expensive decoration of the room is a tribute to the rising fortunes of this mercantile class. The overall effect is one of 'eine beinahe an Glanz streifende Wohlhabenheit' (p.152). (The similarity to the stage directions to Act I of Hauptmann's *Vor Sonnenaufgang* is striking). Ring's wife is 'scheu und verlegen' and their daughters rather forward and uncouth, so that they scarcely match up to their social pretensions, which are clearly based on money — a fact which jars on the established aristocracy.

But it is the characters' speech which constitutes the most revealing part of their presentation, and to that aspect of composition Fontane assigned supreme importance. Our next chapter is devoted to an analysis of its role in *Effi Briest*.

7. Conversational Variations

Fontane's skill as a writer of dialogue has been widely acclaimed: he was himself acutely conscious of his excellence in this sphere. 'Wie soll man die Menschen sprechen lassen? Ich bilde mir ein, daß nach dieser Seite hin eine meiner *Forcen* liegt, und daß ich auch die Besten (unter den Lebenden die Besten) auf diesem Gebiet übertreffe', he wrote to his daughter Meta on 24 August 1892. Many dimensions of this skill reveal themselves in *Effi Briest*.

Fontane's aim is to catch the natural speech mode of his characters, helping them to come to life as credible, realistic, individual figures. In some of his novels, notably *Frau Jenny Treibel* (1892), conversation occupies the major part of the narrative: in *Effi Briest* it is not quite so dominant an element, but it still constitutes a principal means of characterisation, of information-giving and of social commentary.

By avoiding the use of indirect speech as far as possible, Fontane achieves a vivid presentation. The very immediacy of direct speech, as it is enacted before us, has a dramatic quality that is basically denied to reported speech. A greater degree of individualisation is made possible, through the reproduction of idiosyncratic features like hesitations, repetitions, grammatical inaccuracies, cliché, colloquialisms, broken sentences and, of course, exclamations. The opening conversation between Effi and her childhood friends is an excellent example (p.10). Effi's implicit acceptance of the social code of her seniors in the matter of qualities required in a male partner, the disconnected flow of thought, the self-assertive vivacity and dismissive unconcern of the young heroine, all this emerges with a dynamism which reported speech could never achieve. Meanwhile, a body of important information is also conveyed to the reader: the impending arrival of Innstetten, his previous association with Frau von Briest, the fact that Effi has already met him and been favourably impressed. The automatic assumption of her father's views ('Weiber weiblich, Männer männlich') is also indicated; and our appetite has been whetted by the promise of further revelations to come.

Fontane's readers thus participate in a developing process, instead of being second-hand witnesses. Perhaps the finest example of this is the crucial conversation between Innstetten and Wüllersdorf, before the challenge to Crampas: Wandrey describes it as the greatest conversation scene in the German novel (*17*, p.285). It has received little analysis in detail, despite the fact that it is a superb example of how Fontane's conversations often embody the intersection of the individual and the corporate, of private and public self. Innstetten, struggling with a force greater than himself, seeks to uphold the freedom of individual choice, and Fontane charts the progress of his surrender. His desperate search for an answer to his dilemma — can any argument be found for the avoidance of a duel — emerges clearly in the questioning and exploring of issues which goes on between the two men. Choice of vocabulary reinforces their need to be convinced by an institutional, almost bureaucratic presentation of the situation ('Paragraphen', 'beurteilen') and both finally concede the supremacy of a social identity, while privately regretting its necessity. It is a *man*-made morality that rules ('Das mit dem Gottesgericht ist ein Unsinn'): under it people are tested and assessed as to the degree and extent of their conformity ('alle Beleidigungen auf ihren Beleidigungsgehalt chemisch zu untersuchen', 'das richtige Quantum Stickstoff', p.237).

We follow the train of Innstetten's developing thoughts: his private self lingers over the *Verjährungstheorie*, his continuing love for Effi and lack of animosity towards Crampas; his inclination is to forgive and forget. Against this are set his countervailing respect for social order and self-esteem; the dangers implicit in having shared his secret with Wüllersdorf; the loss of personal integrity if he does not act. The debate issues in the final emergence of the resigned acceptance that is Wüllersdorf's: 'Ich finde es furchtbar, daß Sie recht haben, aber Sie *haben* recht' (p.237). The key word throughout is *trotzdem*, for there are contradictions on all sides. In these few pages of conversation a kind of catharsis is undergone by characters and reader alike. The very personal quality of the dilemma comes across in the numerous asides and semi-apologetic interruptions, as in the statement: 'Verzeihen Sie, daß ich Ihnen solche Vorlesung halte, die schließlich doch nur sagt, was sich jeder selber hundertmal gesagt hat' (p.236).

At a quite different level is the to-and-fro of repartee between Crampas and Effi. Their excursion to the dunes culminates in a verbal sparring match that is presented without commentary or description, like dialogue from a play. It moves lightly and swiftly, but deep undercurrents run beneath the surface, as for instance in Crampas' adaptation of the folksong motif *Die Gedanken sind frei*. The train of his thought finally reveals itself in his sensitivity to Effi's mention of lips (pp.135-36).

The use of speech in the service of social commentary is demonstrated particularly in the instance of Sidonie von Grasenabb. This straight-laced and crabbed spinster voices her condemnation of the younger generation and contemporary mores at Oberförster Ring's reception. Her expressions 'Kokette', 'richtige Schule', 'heutzutage', 'Fürsorge für junge Seelen', 'obliegt', are all loaded terms and tell us more about Sidonie than about the criticised Cora Ring. They derive from a starchy, patriarchal tradition of which she is the living representative (p.153).

Many more and widely varied instances of Fontane's skill at presenting speech could be listed, ranging from the fashionable but superficial repartee of Effi's military cousin Dagobert, or tense — or playful — exchanges between Effi and Innstetten, to the dynamic exuberance of Marietta Trippelli or the speculative exchanges between Herr von Briest and his wife. There are 'set-piece' speeches too, including that category in which Fontane excelled — the after-dinner toast.

Briest's toast on Effi's engagement is reported in indirect speech, an unusual procedure for Fontane. Briest is not a man of many words: he does not adjust very easily to this 'Feierlich-keitsrolle', and his wife generally finds him 'ein wenig prosaisch' (p.19). But he does rise to the occasion as the traditional ice-cream is served at the end of the meal, to indulge in the display of verbal dexterity which was *de rigueur* at such moments: Innstetten's name, Geert, is identified as a word denoting a tall, slim tree, while the name Effi calls to mind 'Efeu', winding herself round her new support in life. Key expressions from the speech are reproduced directly by Fontane, so that we get its general flavour. At its conclusion, Briest is inclined to agree with his wife that he is perhaps better to leave poetic images alone. A short scene, but it provides telling glimpses of character.

The toast to Oberförster Ring, proposed by Baron von Güldenklee, is a very different matter. The content of this speech is given literally, for it is charged with hidden allusions. (See the masterly analysis by H.H. Remak in *Jolles*, pp.550-62.) The statutory play on words is first indulged in, demonstrating the qualities of Güldenklee's linguistic wit, as he expounds various connotations of the term 'Ring', moving over to a per-functory demonstration of his cultural knowledge with the reference to Lessing's parable of the three rings in his *Nathan der Weise*. Here, however, a new note is struck, with anti-Semitic, anti-liberal sentiments, highly dismissive of this 'classic' Lessing and a veiled reference to recent political unrest in Germany, which had been blamed on Jews, liberals and socialist sympathisers. The soul of wit being brevity (and his point being forcibly made), Güldenklee concludes on a rousing crescendo, in which he not only salutes the merits of Ring but also of the traditional Prussian spirit of the region. His concluding words are a paean of praise to the old Prussian state (*not* the newly-founded Germany of 1871) with its King and Church, as he sees it embodied still 'in unserm altpommerschen Kessiner Kreise'. His inspired audience breaks spontaneously into the singing of the *Preußenlied*, in a closing gesture of local patriotic fervour (pp.154-55). A masterly piece of social commentary, and a highly entertaining scene at the same time.

In sharp contrast to such scenes are the interior monologues. Mostly they are given to Effi, though Innstetten also feels the need to reflect on his actions as he returns from the duel with Crampas. We rehearse with him the many issues that pass through his mind, their sequence and intensity captured so much more tellingly than could be achieved by their simple authorial cataloguing. The desperate seeking to justify his killing of Crampas is reflected in the long sequence of questions he asks himself, as he moves from comparative self-assurance to the feeling that he has acted wrongly and it is now too late for remedies (pp.242-43). Several of his sentences break off, as he pursues a train of thought into speculative infinities: if only he had killed Crampas out of actual hatred ... now he will have to send Effi away and ruin both their lives ... there are many marriages which manage to persist, even in unhappiness ... This is not the public Innstetten we have learned to know, but a man full of hesitations and misgivings.

Effi's interior monologues likewise arise from states of acute anxiety. Only half-articulated thoughts are formulated, as for instance when we find her at her dressing-table, filled with growing apprehension over her relationship with Crampas and finally admitting her helplessness (p.169). Through this medium, a tradition that goes back to the dramatic monologue, but is capable of more extended development in the novel, character is most profoundly revealed, for here there is no one to deceive, impress or persuade, unless it be the speaker's own self.

More crucial still is Effi's self-reproach after Innstetten's promotion, as she struggles with her sense of shame though not of guilt. We follow the to-and-fro of her thoughts, as she moves from fear of discovery to other emotions: shame, principally over the deception she has to engage in: *Lüge*, so foreign to her basic nature, has become part of her life. The inadequate sense of guilt over her misdeed is then pondered: why *can't* she feel more guilty? The moral self in Effi protests against her 'crime', finding only condemnation for her deed, whether in general or in individual terms (p.219). This soliloquy ends with anticipations of eternal damnation, according to the religious beliefs in which Effi has been educated; it comes close to being a prayer, and the closing reference to 'Gottes Barmherzigkeit' is not inappropriate.

A half-way stage between straight authorial reporting and the form of the interior monologue is represented by *erlebte Rede*. Here, a passage of authorial narration is interrupted by snatches of a character's own thoughts, but without there being any change of grammatical form to signal the presence of a different voice. The perspective thus shifts, for short moments, to that of the person concerned, as unspoken thoughts obtrude in direct pronouncements, reflecting their intensity. Effi's departure from Kessin provides one such change of narrative perspective: 'Effi gedachte des Tages, wo sie, vor jetzt gerade Fünfvierteljahren, im offenen Wagen am Ufer eben dieses Breitlings hin entlanggefahren war. *Eine kurze Spanne Zeit, und das Leben oft so still und einsam. Und doch, was war alles seitdem geschehen!*' Effi's inner thoughts break to the surface in the italicised words (my italics), to suggest most poignantly her feelings at this moment (p.191).

Effi is, very appropriately, the person whose subjective states are most represented in this way. On the evening of Innstetten's first absence from Kessin, she faces a challenge: 'Arme Effi', reports Fontane, 'Wie sollte sie den Abend verbringen? Früh zu Bett, das war gefährlich, dann wachte sie auf und konnte nicht wieder einschlafen und horchte auf alles. Nein, erst recht müde werden und dann ein fester Schlaf, das war das beste' (p.69). The avoidance of the conditional form of the verb, which reported speech would require; the direct 'früh zu Bett' and 'nein', and absence of the finite verb in the second sentence are characteristic of *erlebte Rede*. Transposed into the present tense of the first person singular, with 'Effi' and 'sie' changed to 'ich's, this would be direct speech.

In the course of his characters' conversations Fontane also provides the reader with information on the preoccupations, activities, tastes and priorities of this social world. Conversation thus becomes an important component in the social commentary in which he is engaged. The choice of idiom, the colloquialisms, the quotations and the cultural references further reinforce these impressions. There are passing references to prominent figures of the day, to political but also theatrical and musical events, to cultural preferences, to favourite restaurants, the preferred walks and public venues — this mainly in the context of Berlin life, for in Kessin restrictions of every kind operate and the range of conversation is similarly greatly narrowed, as is, of course, the scope for social occasions.

Often Fontane's characters are seen to use words to obscure meaning; denying, as it were, the very function of language (*4*, p.72; *8*, p.374). Inconsequentialities are spoken, for fear of revealing personal feelings or private commitment. The individual thus remains isolated even in the midst of society. Such 'withholding' of commitment can occur between husband and wife also, as Effi discovers to her cost.

The charge has been made that in his late works Fontane allows certain characters to adopt his own digressive and casual mode of speech, so that they lose in differentiation and individuality. There is some truth in this criticism, so far as it is related to public conversation: it could even be intended as an indication of the stereotypes with which the polite social world operates. Considerable differentiation is nevertheless achieved between the individual figures of *Effi Briest*. Crampas uses uncomplicated constructions, speaks freely, adopting cultural references and proverbs, and is fond of challenging formulations ('Wer gerade gewachsen ist, ist für Leichtsinn': 'Junge Frauen glauben vieles nicht'). His literary tastes tend towards the cynical (he is fond of Heine) and the hazardous and bold, as evidenced by the ballad. Innstetten prefers lengthy sentences; he speaks slowly and carefully, as though requiring his listeners to note his words, many of which are foreign in origin, with almost bureaucratic insistence. He seems devoid of genuine literary interests and his conversation is lacking in cultural allusions. Effi's speech is energetic, disconnected, almost childlike and highly derivative; she prefers simple, religious themes, romantic stories or social novels (p.198). These — especially the religious themes — are attuned specifically to her personal needs. Herr von Briest is cautious, easy-going and speaks in short, non-committal sentences punctuated by genial interjections. Dagobert is almost a caricature of the young military officer, with his fashionable jargon and smart clichés.

8. *The Crampas Letters*

A very special form of communication is constituted by letters. Many letters are written in the course of *Effi Briest*, occasioned by a wide variety of circumstances. Those written to Effi by Major von Crampas constitute a special case and deserve consideration in their own right.

Whereas the real-life 'Effi, komm' incident sparked off the genesis of Fontane's novel, it is on the discovery of the clandestine correspondence that the action itself turns. These letters become a catalyst for our understanding of many of the characters and of society's code of values. They represent an element of economy in the narrative, as well as helping Fontane to steer his novel away from the erotic, which was never his concern: 'Die berühmten "Schilderungen" (der Gipfel der Geschmacklosigkeit) vermeide ich freilich — aber Effis Brief an Crampas und die drei mitgeteilten Zettel von Crampas an Effi, die sagen doch alles' (letter of 12 June 1895).

What *do* these letters tell the reader? Firstly and obviously they expose an intimate relationship between Effi and Crampas. This is a total and shattering revelation to Innstetten — much more than to the reader, for Fontane has in some degree forewarned the latter, who has witnessed a carefully orchestrated campaign by Crampas, leading to an overt declaration of his feelings for Effi in the sleigh episode. Effi has also written a farewell letter to an unidentified person, self-reproachfully terminating an obviously close relationship; and she has delivered it to an isolated house near the dunes where she has recently been in the habit of taking solitary walks. She has been strangely guilt-ridden since leaving Kessin: we have 'overheard' a number of anxious soliloquies and seen her almost 'betray herself' in crucial conversations with her husband. Of all this, Innstetten is oblivious, a fact which helps us to sympathise with his initial complete confusion on discovering the letters.

Innstetten, the man of principle and social propriety, is shown at a distinct disadvantage when overtaken by his emotions. It is the cerebral decision to go ahead with the duel that nevertheless prevails. This stark revelation of the springs of Innstetten's character only becomes possible through the extreme and irrational situation which arises with his finding of the letters.

More fundamentally still, the letters provide us with the vital facts of Effi's act of deception. Fontane clearly did not wish to allocate a sizeable part of his novel to the details of the seduction. What information, precisely, does he give us in these letters? Innstetten has selected just three for a second, closer reading. 'Es schien, daß er gleich beim ersten Durchlesen ein paar davon ausgewählt und obenauf gelegt hatte', Fontane tells us (p.232). 'Es schien, daß ...' is appropriate indeed, for the author is concealing his own hand here. The three letters which Innstetten now re-reads are by no means a random selection. They are arranged in the correct temporal sequence; they relate to the key moments in the affair; and they convey all the information that it is necessary for the reader to possess. What lies in the remaining letters is never revealed: it is in fact totally unimportant.

The extracts take up considerably less than a page of the novel, but their implications are immense. They relate to three separate, progressive stages of Effi's liaison with Crampas. The first note is obviously an early one, perhaps the very first, and it establishes the basis on which the two are to meet, giving a time of day and a place; the 'wieder' indicates that at least one encounter has already taken place. The locations 'Dünen' and 'Mühle' have featured in the story so regularly that we need no more substantial indication of the venue: 'können wir uns ruhig sprechen, das Haus ist abgelegen genug' (p.232) emphasises the need for secrecy, while reassuring Effi with its 'genug'. Effi does indeed appear to need some reassurance and the following lines fulfil this function, encouraging her to assert her claim on the world. The concluding lines are pure Crampas: the attack on the established order, questioning its validity (the word 'gelten' is a crucial term thoughout the novel) and authority, is in stark contrast to Innstetten's implicit faith in *Ordnung* and *Gesetz*. It is aimed at Effi's delight in danger and her spontaneity as a person.

The next letter shows the extent to which Crampas succeeded — and finds him already getting out of his depth. Effi, no longer able to bear her existence in Kessin, has identified Crampas as a mode of escape. With adolescent naivety (she is still only eighteen years old) she believes in the simple expedient of flight, in the company of the man who has proclaimed his passion for her and his scorn for society's conventions. But Crampas stresses his ties and responsibilities: he has duties towards wife and daughters, and accepts the social commitment he has made. The only escape he envisages lies in subterfuge and frivolity: 'Leichtsinn ist das Beste, was wir haben' (p.233). Not exactly a moral stance, nor even a co-ordinated response; more a philosophy of opportunism. In case Effi is disposed to recrimination, he quickly shrugs off all personal responsibility: 'Alles ist Schicksal. Es hat so sein sollen'. The carefully contrived seduction is put down to a trick of fate.

The third note indicates the end of their liaison. Effi is escaping from Kessin — by virtue not of Crampas' guile but of her deceived husband's merit. A farewell meeting is proposed by Crampas and there is some self-pity at her departure: yet he is glad it is all over. Another act of fate is now requiring their separation, just as it supposedly brought them together.

The three notes differ in their style and tone. The first is masterful, encouraging; its message coherent and consistently constructed, the syntactical groups lengthy but smooth-flowing. The imperative tone prevails. The second note is more disjointed, unsure, almost apologetic. The syntactical groups are noticeably shorter and more broken, and the whole concludes with a question mark. The writer here seeks to reassure himself just as much as the recipient. The third extract (and these are *only* extracts, crucial passages from longer communications, phrases that make the chief impact on Innstetten, and thus a kind of *innere Rede*) is somewhat calmer again. The rhythmic pattern is more balanced, the statement more articulate and connected. It concludes with a lengthy sentence, in which we can feel the tensions ebbing away in a flow of words, as resignation sets in. The Crampas whom we encounter in these extracts is a different person from the debonair, suave figure we once knew. He has travelled to the brink, but turns back now to society.

But where, in time, are we to place this third communication from Crampas? The note clearly implies his knowledge that Effi will soon be leaving Kessin. Effi must therefore have let him know of Innstetten's promotion immediately after the latter's return from Berlin. Indeed, she must have done so with some haste. Crampas' note proposes one further meeting, and in *Du* terms. The exact moment of her departure is not yet known to him — nor indeed even to Effi — and therefore has to be indicated in a further note, that intriguing letter to an unknown person which Effi writes on the very eve of leaving Kessin. She still finds time to slip away and deliver it at their secret rendez-vous — the only ever explicit indication by Fontane of its location, but long in advance of the *revelation* of their secret liaison, with its documentary evidence. There is a definite suggestion that Effi did not concede that last meeting, and that this letter is her actual farewell to Crampas, who is here distanced by the use of the formal pronoun *Sie* and the requested vow of silence and non-intervention. She shows considerable generosity of spirit by assuming the entire burden of guilt.

In the preceding pages, Fontane has been indulging in some subtle adumbration, in the conversation between Effi and Roswitha. Effi has just returned from a lonely walk: she is tired, hungry and her hair is wet. She reproves Roswitha for flirting with Kruse, the coachman, pointing out that he is a married man: 'Das kann nie was werden' she concludes (p.176). She then proceeds to ask Roswitha, surprisingly for the first time ever, about the latter's 'fall from grace' and its consequences. 'Ach, gnädigste Frau', interjects Roswitha, 'die Heil'ge Mutter Gottes bewahre Sie vor solchem Elend'. Effi's reaction is instant: 'Effi fuhr auf und sah Roswitha mit großen Augen an. Aber sie war mehr erschrocken als empört'. Is Fontane anticipating the consequences that are to flow from the discovered letters?

Criticism of Prussian society is another function of the episode. The reaction of Effi's parents, in their rejection of their much cherished, but 'sinful' daughter, 'weil wir Farbe bekennen' (p.255) is an indictment of a society that places public conformity before compassion. Further criticism is represented in the person of Frau von Zwicker: '— erst selber Zettel und Briefe schreiben und dann auch noch die des anderen aufbewahren! Wozu gibt es Öfen und Kamine?' (p.258). The *Geheimrätin*'s incredulity not only suggests her own mode of procedure, but also throws Effi's behaviour into kinder light. The vital requirement of this society is not so much to avoid sinning, but rather to avoid being caught. Most of the characters in the novel are in the end called upon to declare their priorities in the wake of Innstetten's discovery of the letters, and reveal more of their true selves in the process.

We still need to ask: why did Effi keep these dangerous letters? She herself never refers to them and offers no explanation for their retention. She certainly did not keep Innstetten's *Brautbriefe* to her, which she found remarkably pedestrian. On her own admission, she never loved Crampas: 'den ich nicht einmal liebte und den ich vergessen hatte, weil ich ihn nicht liebte' (p.275). They lie at the bottom of her work-box, under a welter of bric-a-brac from the past (p.229) and Roswitha remembers that they were tightly tied together, without a bow, as though finished with (p.246). Effi's failure to destroy them could be seen as a token of her simple and guileless mind. They were a part of her past, perhaps 'etwas Apartes' to be treasured, now forgotten, and automatically transported from Kessin among her other possessions.

Fontane himself stresses the fascination with guilt which they represent: 'Ja, die nicht verbrannten Briefe in 'Effi'! Unwahrscheinlich ist es gar nicht. Dergleichen kommt immerzu vor. Die Menschen können sich nicht trennen von dem, woran ihre Schuld haftet. Unwahrscheinlich ist es nicht, aber es ist leider trivial' (letter of 24 April 1896).

That the discovery of the letters is delayed by six or more years is a masterly stroke by Fontane. Use of the principle of *Verjährung* thus becomes a weapon in his critique of society. Innstetten's agonising sums it up: 'Zehn Jahre verlangen noch ein Duell, und da heißt es Ehre, und nach elf Jahren oder vielleicht schon bei zehneinhalb heißt es Unsinn. Die Grenze, die

Grenze. Wo ist sie?' (p.243). A society that has to ask itself questions of this nature, on whose answer literally issues of life and death depend, is clearly in a moral no man's land. Fontane pinpoints the agonising clash of private and public worlds in this search for a frontier between emotion and social checks and balances.

One structural effect of the letters is to break the smooth forward flow of the narrative. They represent a moment of balance, being both retrospective in that they look back to events that are completed, and also prospective in the sense that their implications cannot be avoided, causing us to consider what must now be done, — an awareness we share with Innstetten. We have here something like the *Wendepunkt* in the structure of a Novelle, the point on which the whole action turns. It comes remarkably late in the story and it puts into reverse the previously developing pattern of relationships, totally frustrating the 'happy ending', seemingly and credibly in prospect. The withheld revelation is a testimony to Fontane's narrative craft: without it we could not have witnessed the struggle of Effi with her conscience and attempts at social reintegration; nor could that crucial conversation between Innstetten and Wüllersdorf have taken place. A flatter and more conventional story would have resulted.

Effi's fall is the product of chance. Even Innstetten's inspection of the letters is done on the whim of the moment, almost absent-mindedly (p.231). The paradox is presented of chance as the operative principle in a carefully regulated social world. The principle that Crampas had saluted so warmly in his letters to Effi does indeed operate, and his death is the ironic proof. Little wonder that he smiles ruefully when the challenge arrives.

Such fatalism is an element of the ballad tradition, of which many aspects are to be found in *Effi Briest*. The Crampas letters themselves contribute to this ballad-like quality. Their crucial message is expressed in compact formulation, little more than key words featuring much of the time, stark and compelling in their concentration on essential detail, all subsidiary matter omitted as digressive. They leap forward from revelation to revelation without comment, the author remaining as inscrutable as any in the ballad tradition. The time has arrived for us to look at the form and structure of Fontane's novel.

9. Form and Style

Certain broad patterns operate in *Effi Briest*. The narrative itself has a circular movement: in Chapter 1 the young Effi plays around the 'Rondell'; in the final chapter she is buried there. Characters attempt in their various ways to move out from their society but are drawn firmly back into it, either willingly or reluctantly. It is society that holds the field at the conclusion, as it did at the outset.

The novel itself consists, as Wandrey has shown (*17*, pp.271-72), of an outer frame, with five introductory chapters (Effi's youth and wedding) and five concluding ones (Effi's decline and death). Within this are set three fairly equally balanced central sections, made up of Chapters 6-14 (Effi's first months in Kessin and the birth of her child), Chapters 15-22 (Crampas' arrival and relationship with Effi) and Chapters 23-31 (promotion to Berlin, the duel and Effi's disgrace).

Time, however, is allocated disproportionately to the different stages of Effi's life. In all, she spends considerably less than two years in Kessin, while in Berlin her life together with Innstetten covers more than six years. From the time of her separation from Innstetten to her death, Effi lives another four years. Yet seventeen chapters are devoted to life in Kessin, nine to their married life in Berlin, and only five to the final four years. Here we find reflected the basic concern of the novel — the presentation of the precise circumstances surrounding Effi's fall. Society judges her in the light of her experiences in Kessin, as she steps forth into life, and these events occupy a dominating place in the novel. The slower and more meticulous pattern of the narrative here is a mirror of the tedium of life in this small Pomeranian town.

Commenting on the almost arcane indication of time dimensions by Fontane, Avery (*18*, pp.36-38) detects a division into six-week periods, some approximate and some quite precisely dated. By still more sophisticated analysis, Avery relates Effi's life to a diurnal rhythm, so that her actual death, between 10 and 11 p.m., relates her to the 'nocturnal' element of the Chinaman. Innstetten on the other hand confuses the timeless challenge to his feelings constituted by Effi's deception, with the mechanical, juridical concept of time represented by *Verjährung*, and opts for the latter.

Effi Briest tends to the lyrical and avoids the dramatic. Confrontation scenes are largely evaded: in particular, no meeting or even exchange of letters occurs between Effi and Innstetten after the discovery of Crampas' letters. Much use is made of symbols, directing the reader's attention away from externals to inward, subjective states, and reducing the importance of factual event. With the closing chapters, an even more lyrical note suffuses the text. The pace slows considerably: dialogue and monologue completely replace action; description and reflection take over from event. All the characters are involved in a coming-to-terms with the past, Innstetten and the Briests just as much as Effi. The novel itself concludes not with Effi's death, but with a conversation: it is open-ended, and it poses questions — questions which take us right back to the opening chapters.

The chapters themselves are by no means equal in length or import. Some are very brief and deal with one crucial incident: four pages for Chapter 31 in which Effi receives news of her banishment; for Chapter 33 just over three pages, devoted to Effi's meeting with her daughter, covering at most three hours' narrated time. The preceding chapter on the other hand is at least three times as long, and covers Effi's life in Berlin since her separation from Innstetten, a period of three years. Chapter 20 is packed with apparently quite disparate elements, which yet have a unity in Effi's subconscious.

Ballad elements occur in Fontane's writing, doubtless a continuing influence from his cultivation of the ballad in younger years. The action often leaps forward from one situation to the next with no narrative material to supply substance to the intervals. Some chapter endings are sudden and abrupt, like the ballad's stanza endings, frequently in the middle of a conversation. The suggestion of uncompleted, continuing action

carries the reader's interest forwards, in the briefest of formulations (Chapters 11, 18, 27).

The considerable role played by uncommented dialogue is
another feature of the ballad tradition. Also common to both is
the psychological interest vested in the supernatural. The author
mostly conceals his own identity, leaving suggestive images to
operate instead. Continuity and cohesion are, on the other hand,
assisted by the use of leitmotifs and the recurrence of scenic
features (see Chapter 6 above). Prefiguration and adumbration
occur too, most generally through the figure of the Chinaman,
but also in such features as the *Hertha Steine* (pp.211, 280) and
their connotations of blood sacrifice, anticipating Effi's own
fate, already prefigured in Frau von Padden's paschal lamb
reference to Effi as 'ein junges Lämmchen, weiß wie Schnee'
(p.204). Fate is represented by external forces which operate
through society, forces which Effi believes she can challenge, yet
which she has from the outset acknowledged, so that a form of
predestination is seen to operate (*2*, pp.30-31).

There are however significant differences from the ballad
tradition. The forward movement of the action is not always
urgent and it can even be set in reverse. Fontane, seeking to
engage the reader's sympathy for Effi, also occasionally slips
into the sentimental manner. We note, in particular, his open
intervention into the narrative, with expressions like 'arme Effi'
(pp.69, 292); while the scene with Pastor Niemeyer, in which
Effi's entry into heaven is assured, sails perilously close to
Kitsch (p.281).

But Fontane is mostly discreet as a narrator, conveying much
of his meaning through metaphors and symbols. The metaphor
of flight is frequently applied to Effi (see Chapter 2) to suggest
her unconstrained manner, culminating in her final: 'mir war,
als flög' ich in den Himmel' (p.281); while the metaphor of
trains expresses her yearning for Hohen-Cremmen. Her sailor
outfit, appropriately resumed on her return to her parents, combines with a complex of metaphors and symbols of water and the
sea ('Teich', 'Flut', 'Dünen', 'Schloon', 'Schiffbruch') to
suggest Effi's affinity with the elemental: this complex extends
to Crampas and Innstetten, reflecting their attitudes to the

unknown (*18*, pp.31-32; *21*, pp.74-75). 'Heliotrop' and 'Platanen' signify respectively the colour and warmth, or the scope for unfettered growth, which Hohen-Cremmen represents for Effi.

Of nature there is little description, unless it be used as backdrop to a particular incident, like the delightful winter sleigh outing to Klein Tantow (Chapter 10), the more frightening encounter with the 'Schloon' and the dark pine-woods (Chapter 19), or the peaceful atmosphere of the sand-dunes and open sea (Chapters 13, 17). Fontane was more concerned with people than with nature, and especially with people in their social context. Nature supplies much of the symbolism, however: woods in particular represent danger to Effi, who avoids them when possible; it is in the 'selva oscura' of sin that Crampas declares his passion for her, shut off from the openness of the night sky (see Bance and Devine in *Jolles*, pp.412 and 547-48).

Theatrical allusions occur throughout the text. Effi, already fascinated by Crampas, takes a part in a play with the significant title, *Ein Schritt vom Wege*. She regards Innstetten's playing on her fear of the 'Spuk' as 'eine Komödie' (p.172); Innstetten sees all life after the duel in 'Komödie' terms, both his own conduct (p.243) and that of Johanna (p.286). The ridiculousness of human posturing is suggested via this theatrical metaphor, so beloved of the nineteenth century.

Through symbol and metaphor, adumbration and prefiguration, by character grouping and contrast, through conversation, monologue and letters, Fontane successfully conceals his own persona, leaving his novel-figures to stand in their own right. In his scrupulous attention to detail, Fontane persuades us of the truth of what he puts before us. Moreover, the understated quality of his narrative — the reliance on implication rather than overt statement — invites us to debate with our own consciences, to form our own judgments.

10. Critical Reception and Literary Assessment

Fontane enjoyed the mostly positive reception which his novel was given. For four or five weeks he did nothing but write letters of thanks to reviewers: 'Ich habe auf die Weise schon wenigstens ein Dutzend ziemlich lange Briefe geschrieben' (19 November 1895 to Friedländer). The first edition of 1895 was followed by two further ones in the same year, and by 1905 the novel was appearing in its sixteenth edition. It was Fontane's first really immediate success, and the only matter that disturbed him was some severe criticism of Innstetten, which he strove in his correspondence to counteract, insisting on Innstetten's basically good qualities.

In letters to relatives and friends he is concerned to stress the importance of the *Verjährungstheorie*, of the Crampas letters and of the *Spuk*, all of which had been largely neglected by the reviewers. He seems also to have been taken aback by the extent to which his novel was construed as an attack on Prussian authoritarianism and is at pains to stress the need for a measure of order and respect for principle within society (e.g. letter of 27 October 1895). All in all, Fontane was not greatly impressed by the perceptiveness of his reviewers: he had, he conceded, received a few really appreciative tributes, but 'dazwischen krabbelt viel Mittelwertiges herum, und von der Majorität der Fälle schweigt des Sängers Höflichkeit' (21 February 1896).

For some time after his death in 1898 Fontane's novels received little serious critical attention, the first notable study being that by Conrad Wandrey, of 1919, which still remains a useful literary biography. This, and M.E. Gilbert, *Das Gespräch in Fontanes Gesellschaftsromanen* (4), stand out in a virtual critical wilderness. This comparative neglect (there are a few honourable exceptions) is no doubt due partly to the rapidly evolving literary tradition of those years, and also to the virtual extinction, in the 1920s, of the society which Fontane had presented in such detail. Neither Expressionism nor *Neue Sachlichkeit* had affinities with that world, and the ensuing cult of *Blut und Boden* even less so. It is only after 1945 that Fontane became the subject of intensive study in his native land, one might almost say for the first time: the Bibliography is some indication of the range and intensity of the subsequent investigation, which has concerned itself especially with *Effi Briest*, as his finest work.

In Britain, matters stood even less favourably. As recently as 1961, Brian Rowley reflected on the fact that not one major work by Fontane existed in English translation; and worse still, that standard and authoritative British histories of the European novel did not even include his name. Much has however changed in the last twenty-five years, bringing Fontane to the close attention of the British public; not least through the showing of Fassbinder's film of *Effi Briest* (1974), finely crafted but sadly inadequate, with suggestions of 'women's liberation' ideology. Many of Fontane's subtleties are lost in a selective presentation of episodes, deliberately excluding the 'action' scenes, in an attempt to distance the viewer, who is supposedly helped thereby to a more critical judgment. Three other film versions exist: *Ein Schritt vom Wege*, by Gustaf Gründgens (1939), *Rosen im Herbst*, by Rudolf Jugert (1956) and one made in the G.D.R. by Wolfgang Luderer in 1969.

Since 1967 an excellent English version of *Effi Briest* exists, in the Penguin Classics series (by Douglas Parmée, translator also of *Unwiederbringlich*, Oxford, 1964); and there has been a succession of highly effective British studies of the writer (see Bibliography). The *Jolles-Festschrift* of 1979 produced a weighty international tribute to our author (and also to this leading British exponent of his work), including several devoted to *Effi Briest*. Other studies have appeared in the *Fontane Blätter*, published since 1965 in Potsdam at the *Fontane Archiv*. The novel itself features on the lists of numerous publishers, and in the Ullstein Verlag in 1983 reached its 159-178 thousandth edition.

Practically all critics concur that *Effi Briest* represents the peak of Fontane's literary achievement. Such was the general opinion among Fontane's contemporaries and so it remains today; even those who have written in a more summary fashion on Fontane usually pause to look more closely at *Effi Briest*. Thus Roy Pascal and J.P. Stern each devote a section of their respective chapters on Fontane to this work, although both of them, in these relatively pioneering English studies, commit minor errors of fact, the latter even consistently mis-spelling Innstetten's name.

Where some treatments of *Effi Briest* have been general in character, other, and especially more recent, studies have proved both more detailed and more sophisticated. Thus D.C. Riechel (*Jolles*, pp.417-427) has suggested influences from Goethe's *Wahlverwandtschaften* (1809), on which Fontane made detailed notes when he read it in 1870, particularly with regard to the conflict within the heroine between her total naturalness and the strictures of the biblical commandments; the fact that Ottilie and Effi are both seventeen is noted, together with their 'child-woman' natures. Both are found to have affinities with the elemental and the instinctive: the air of decadence and the incessant grooming of nature in Goethe's work find parallels in the social nervousness and pscyhological repressions in *Effi Briest*. Both women, fashioned by society in the image of the 'Mary' figure, fail in spite of themselves. Such parallelisms may be found, but there is much else that differentiates the two works, which belong essentially to their own historical periods and arise from greatly differing patterns of motivation, Goethe's work deriving from pscyhological speculation on the motives for human behaviour, Fontane's from a real-life event, recreated in the image of his times.

Admiration for Fontane's work becomes more qualified when he is considered in the broader context of European writing. Comparison with Flaubert's *Madame Bovary* (1857) and Tolstoy's *Anna Karenina* (1877) immediately suggests itself. All three are novels of a wife's adultery, but approached in radically different manner. Tolstoy's novel is one of acute pscyhological analysis, the study of a woman torn between passion and duty, between the openly avowed love for a man which she in unable to renounce and her awareness of its destructive impact on others, including her husband, her son, and even her lover, Vronsky, tormented by the raging of her conflicting allegiances. Tolstoy's heroine faces a challenge of an essentially moral character: her behaviour is publicly known, familiar to all, and the decision is hers entirely whether to opt for love or duty — alternatives so irreconcilable yet so acutely experienced that she is destroyed by the sheer impossibility of choosing. Effi, by contrast, faces a more muted dilemma, in that her secret adultery is an affront to the established code, in which she herself implicitly believes; her final acceptance of her fate indicates her acceptance of this code. No agonising conflict of principles here, rather the elegiac record of a delightfully natural but somewhat weak-willed woman seeking to reintegrate herself into a world whose *raison d'être* she only half comprehends. J.P. Stern (*16*, pp.316-339) sees society as the law-giver here. Yet to see Effi's struggle in purely social terms, denying it a moral dimension, as Stern's analysis does, is to ignore the fight with her sense of shame and her rejection of all women who assume a guiltless stance in her kind of situation.

Emma Bovary's is a different kind of social rebellion: here the avowed intention is to escape the deadeningly restrictive pall of a hidebound provincial town in a naive craving for self-realisation in sensual pleasure. 'J'ai un amant' is her cry of triumph. Emma keeps her secret, but finds herself the victim of others' ruthlessness and her own illusions, finally so despairing of retrieving herself that the only remedy is found in suicide. Flaubert passes judgment on both society and Emma, remaining very much the objective reporter of events, so that he could, at his trial for indecent publication, claim to have written not an indulgent book but rather an improving one. No sympathetic figures surround Emma in her narrow provincial world, her wooden husband does not even begin to understand her, and crass materialism confronts her on every side. Yet Emma's actions are seen with a critical eye too, as Flaubert records her progressive decline, a process documented by such symbolic devices as her successive encounters with the beggar.

Flaubert's caustic observation of the rising forces of the bourgeoisie in mid-nineteenth-century France is very different

from the even-handed presentation of the local gentry by
Fontane, even though in *Effi Briest* the more desirable
characters operate rather on the periphery than at the epicentre,
or tend to belong to the older generation. Flaubert is concerned
with a culture that is trapped between the uncompromising
demands of religion and of science and is on the brink of total
ethical collapse. He condemns the church which offers Emma no
help, and the hollow values of the free professions, with their
false idols and vicious denial of the world of beauty. The
triumph goes to Homais and Lheureux, who represent the new
attitudes of cold science and ruthless exploitation.

Fontane on the other hand does not reject summarily the
society which he presents, seeing that social forms are essential
for the preservation of civilised conduct and personal security.
Adultery endangers the *Ordnung* of life: Crampas' transgression
of this order is a threat to human relationships and their
permanence in a recognised and civilised institution, which is
marriage. The old values *can* be reasserted positively; new
understanding of them is required, not new standards and
structures.

Fontane's provincialism and narrowness of range are revealed
when comparison is made with *Anna Karenina*. Tolstoy's is a
work on a truly grand scale, historically, geographically, socially
and intellectually. Where Fontane presents an enclosed little
world located around Berlin and its region, Tolstoy's novel
seems to take in the whole of Russian society with its
tremendous sweep — from toiling peasantry to royal count,
from communist agitator to imperialist minister, from
harvesting reapers to the supreme sophistication of Moscow and
St Petersburg; and where Fontane speculates about Bismarck,
Tolstoy muses on God and ultimate realities.

Effi Briest experiences none of the extreme passion that
wracks both Tolstoy's and Flaubert's heroines, seeming indeed
almost passionless by comparison. Numerous critics have com-
mented in this respect on Fontane's habitual avoidance of the
erotic — a practice of which he himself was fully conscious: this
he saw as the concern of the trivial novel of his day. He wrote to
Heilborn on 24 November 1895:

Sie sind ... auch einverstanden damit, daß ich, in den intrikaten Situationen, der Phantasie des Lesers viel über-lasse; dies anders zu machen wäre mir ganz unmöglich, und ich würde totale Dunkelheiten immer noch einer Gas-glühlichtbeleuchtung von Dingen vorziehen, die, selbst wenn ihre Darstellung geglückt ist (ein sehr selten vorkommender Fall), immer noch mißglückt wirken.

Fontane is clearly aware of his stengths and weaknesses; his heroine appears emotionally somewhat anaemic in consequence, and the clash of opposed forces less dramatic. But the point is well made by Müller-Seidel (*8*, pp.370-71) that Innstetten is equally passionless; for in both of them society has seen to the damping down of any excess of emotion. The judgment is thus passed, in the last resort, on society, not the individual. 'Daher', concludes Müller-Seidel, 'sind alle die Werke Fontanes nicht am "klassischen" Eheroman Stendhals, Flauberts oder Tolstoys zu messen, wie es geschieht, wenn man die dort dargestellte Leiden-schaft zum Maßstab des Urteilens macht'. Fontane's figures are 'halbe Helden im leidenschaftslosen Eheroman der bloßen Liebelei' (*8*, p.371). Each novelist reflects the historical character of his period. Fontane's realism consists in his having parted company with the earlier nineteenth-century tradition of the *Leidenschaftsroman*, with its tragic-dramatic treatment of its matter, which had started to distance it from ordinary life. Fontane's story is an everyday one, 'wie hundert andre mehr', as he himself described it (21 February 1896). The situation of the young woman married off to an older husband had not only been presented in earlier works of Fontane himself (*L'Adultera, Cécile*) but was a common theme in European literature, from the eighteenth century down to *A Month in the Country* (1871) by Turgenev — a writer greatly admired by Fontane. Fontane places his story firmly in a Prussian setting: this affects most profoundly his presentation of the husband.

Social forces reduce Innstetten to a condition of *Halbheit* — the denial of his true instincts and an impassive conformity. He is thus a representative figure of this times. Other critics have likewise referred to Innstetten's *Halbheit*, and Bance sees it

indeed as a characteristic of many of Fontane's male pro-
tagonists (*Jolles*, pp.405ff.). For Bance, it is a sign of the
impossibility of heroic action in the post-Napoleonic era and
after the failures of 1848, which gave rise to a sense of
frustration and ineffectuality and half-hearted surrender to the
powers-that-be, perhaps recognised in the Hegelian image of the
state. The era of the passive hero is thus inaugurated, expressed
more sharply in the work of Fontane's contemporary, Wilhelm
Raabe, whose figures move to the fringes of society in a seeking
to preserve their identity and integrity; it eventually finds its
extreme expression in the figure of the outsider and the drop-
out. For Fontane's era, the wish for integration is still
paramount, but a high price must be accepted in terms of
individuality. For Degering (*2*, pp.44ff.) the 'verdoppelt'
character is the result, the category including Effi herself as well
as Crampas and Marietta Trippelli, all partaking of the quality
of *Halbheit* in that their private challenge to society is balanced
and rendered safe by their public assertion of the validity of
society's rules.

The achievement of Fontane is, in the last resort, to have led
the German novel back into the mainstream of European
literature, and in *Effi Briest* the triumph is registered clearly. He
has cast off the fascination with the *Bildungsroman* (novel of
personal development) that had held sway for so long in
Goethe's wake and that of the Romantics: he has escaped from
the almost obsessive concern with the bourgeois and his inner
tensions, rooted in the narrowing confines of a provincial
German setting (e.g. Otto Ludwig's *Zwischen Himmel und
Erde*, 1856). Above all, he has broken free from preoccupation
with the philosophical construing of life and the search for
private systems of belief, all of them factors that kept the
German novel in a channel of its own (see *23*, loc. cit.). In terms
of his own work, *Effi Briest* marks a progression too: Effi is a
far more complex and delicately balanced figure than her earlier
formulation, Melanie van den Straaten (*L'Adultera*, 1882), a
work that parallels in many respects the complications that
occur in the later one, but which resolves them in much simpler
and more conciliatory terms. *Effi Briest* presents men and

women with all their virtues and frailties, devoid of all pretence to set up systems of philosophy and observed 'sur le vif'. Fontane's contemporaries admitted to recognising their own reflection in his work.

Thomas Mann, another 'European' German and in many ways Fontane's literary heir, accorded him due recognition on the occasion of the unveiling of the memorial to Fontane in the Berlin Zoological Gardens in May, 1910, seeing him virtually as the father of the modern German novel and anticipator of much of his own literary technique: 'Und er ist unser Vater...' Only six years separate Fontane's novel from Thomas Mann's *Buddenbrooks*, which have more in common than the name of Crampas' second at the duel.

Select Bibliography

A. BOOKS

1. Bance, Alan, *Theodor Fontane: the Major Novels* (Cambridge, New York: Cambridge University Press, 1982).
2. Degering, Thomas, *Das Verhältnis von Individuum und Gesellschaft in Fontanes 'Effi Briest' und Flauberts 'Madame Bovary'* (Bonn: Bouvier, 1978).
3. Garland, H.B., *The Berlin Novels of Theodor Fontane* (Oxford, New York: Oxford University Press, 1980).
4. Gilbert, M.E., *Das Gespräch in Fontanes Gesellschaftsromanen*, Palaestra Nr 174 (Leipzig: Mayer & Müller, 1930).
5. Kahrmann, Cordula, *Das Idyll im Roman: Theodor Fontane* (Munich: Fink Verlag, 1973).
6. Mittenzwei, Ingrid, *Die Sprache als Thema: Untersuchungen zu Fontanes Gesellschaftsromanen*, Frankfurter Beiträge zur Germanistik, Bd 12 (Berlin: Gehlen, 1970).
7. Martini, Fritz, *Deutsche Literatur im bürgerlichen Realismus*, 2nd edition (Stuttgart: Metzler, 1964), pp.737-800.
8. Müller-Seidel, Walter, *Theodor Fontane: soziale Romankunst in Deutschland* (Stuttgart: Metzler, 1975).
9. Pascal, Roy, *The German Novel* (Manchester: University Press, 1956).
10. Remak, Joachim, *The Gentle Critic: Theodor Fontane and German Politics* (New York: Syracuse University Press, 1964).
11. Reuter, H.-H., *Theodor Fontane* (Leipzig: Reclam, 1969).
12. Richter, Karl, *Resignation: eine Studie zum Werk Theodor Fontanes* (Stuttgart: Kohlhammer, 1966).
13. Robinson, A.R., *Theodor Fontane: an Introduction to the Man and his Work* (Cardiff: University of Wales Press, 1976).
14. Sasse, H.-C., *Theodor Fontane: an Introduction to the Novels and Novellen* (Oxford: Blackwell, 1968).
15. Schillemeit, Jost, *Theodor Fontane: Geist und Kunst seines Alterswerks* (Zurich, Atlantis Verlag, 1961).
16. Stern, J.P., *Re-interpretations* (London: Thames and Hudson, 1964).
17. Wandrey, Conrad, *Theodor Fontane* (Munich: Beck, 1919).

B. ARTICLES

18. Avery, George C., 'The Chinese Wall: Fontane's Psychograph of Effi Briest', in Weimar, K.S. (ed.), *Views and Reviews of Modern German Literature: Festschrift für A.D. Klarmann* (Munich: Delp, 1974).

19. Carter, T.E., 'A Leitmotif in Fontane's "Effi Briest"', in *German Life and Letters*, N.S.10, 1956-57, 38-42.

20. Garland, H.B., 'Theodor Fontane', in *German Men of Letters*, Vol.I (London: Wolff, 1961), 217-33.

21. Gilbert, M.E., 'Fontanes "Effi Briest"', in *Deutschunterricht 11* (1959), Heft 4, 63-75.

22. Radcliffe, S., '"Effi Briest" and the Crampas Letters', in *German Life and Letters*, N.S. 39, 1985-86, 148-60.

23. Rowley, B.A., 'Theodor Fontane: a German novelist in the European Tradition?', in *German Life and Letters*, N.S.15, 1961-62, 72-88.

Useful articles are also to be found in the collection: *Formen realistischer Erzählkunst: Festschrift for Charlotte Jolles* ed. by J. Thunecke (Nottingham: Sherwood Press, 1979).

For a comprehensive review of research carried out on Fontane, see: Charlotte Jolles, *Theodor Fontane*: Realien zur Literatur, 2nd edition (Stuttgart: Metzler, 1976).